# It All Started with a Song

COMPILED, EDITED & ILLUSTRATED BY
## DAVID LIVERETT
*with Judy Spencer Nelon*

Other books by David Liverett:

When Hope Shines Through

Faith for the Journey

Love, Bridges of Reconciliation

and

Oh, to be in Miss Collier's class again!
Christie Smith Stephens and David Liverett

Chinaberry House
P. O. Box 505
Anderson, Indiana 46015-0505
www.2Lights.com

ISBN 0-9742410-1-6
Printed in the United States of America

# DEDICATION

Dedicated to the memory of Joel Hull and Zella Hull Warren,
from whom I learned much about God's love and was
encouraged to sing bass in the choir at the
Austinville Church of God in Decatur, Alabama.

# Old Friends

Words by Gloria Gaither
Music by William J. Gaither and J. D. Miller

*Chorus*

Old friends — after all of these years, just
Old friends – through the laughter and tears
Old friends – What a find! What a priceless treasure!
Old friends – like a rare piece of gold
Old friends – make it great to grow old
  (brought me in from the cold; Christmas version)

Oh, God must have known
That some days on our own
We would lose our will to go on –
That's why He sent friends like you along.

Old friends — yes, you've always been there,
My old friends — we've had more than our share —
Old friends — I'm a rich millionaire in old friends.

*Verse*

A phone call, a letter, a pat on the back,
  or a "Hey, I just dropped by to say . . ."
A hand when we're down, a loan when we just couldn't pay —
A song or a story, a rose from the florist,
  a note that you happened to send—
Out of the blue just to tell us that you're still our friend
*Repeat Chorus*

# FOREWORD

When Bill and I first came to know David Liverett, he was a young struggling artist with a keen eye for layout and design. We were young English teachers writing songs and hoping, on shoestring, to publish collections of our songs and release garage recordings of them. We wanted to make our work look as attractive and professional as possible.

So it was that we first worked with David Liverett on design and layout. Because of his commercial art, David was always around Christian artists and authors, designing book covers, record jackets, and promotional materials.

Even then, aside from his commercial artwork, he was doing lovely line drawings of his babies. He went on to draw historic lighthouses, old churches and a collection of bridges of the Midwest, particularly covered bridges of Indiana. We asked him to do a collage of line-drawings of our three little grandsons, a piece we treasure to this day.

When Bill began gathering gospel music artists together to informally sing the songs we all loved, David would run by the studio to simply enjoy the happening. He began to get acquainted with some of these singers he had not met before and as a result, was drawn to the finished videos.

This book brings the two David Liveretts together: the one that works with artists and the one who creates lovely line-drawings, this time in the form of portraits of the artists themselves. I know you're going to enjoy this collection of sketches — both artistic and biographical of many of the Homecoming artists you've come to love through their music. And at the same time, you get a peak at David Liverett — both sides of him!

— Gloria Gaither

# TABLE OF CONTENTS

# INTRODUCTION

**M**y dad always loved good music. Recently an older first cousin of mine was showing me where my dad grew up. We were travelling the back roads of north Alabama near the village of Anderson. Also in the car were another cousin from my mother's side of the family, my brother who was making a map locating all the houses that my folks had called home, and my wife, Avis. "Here is where the house stood that Uncle Monroe and Mother used to hike through the woods to hear the Grand Ole Opry. They would hurry home and try to imitate the sound." Joyce was telling me something that I didn't know about my dad, although I knew his family had musical talent. I have an old photo of my dad's family standing out in front of the old homeplace. In the picture some of his fifteen siblings are holding musical instruments.

Growing up in Decatur, Alabama, in the 40s and 50s, I still remember Dad, Buford Brewer, and O.T. Terry making music on our front porch because Dad loved good music. One of the songs they would play was "I'm Using My Bible for a Roadmap." He even rigged up a holder for his harmonica so he could play it while he played the guitar. He and Mom bought my brother and sister a Silvertone guitar and a mandolin for Christmas one year. I think it was the same Christmas I received a hand-me-down bike that Dad repainted red. As it turned out, Dad's musical talent died with him. My brother ended up in the space industry and my sister worked in the field of insurance. I am the youngest child and I leaned toward the visual arts.

Our family would go to *All Night Singings* when they were nearby, usually in the high school. I don't remember that the concerts lasted *all* night but they did leave a lasting impression. My memory of the singers was that they wore matching suits and had slicked-back hair and pencil-thin mustaches. We would stay to listen through encore after encore. In 1952, we went to the Ryman

Auditorium. I remember that we were seated under the balcony and someone spilt a Coca-Cola down onto our pew.

After graduating from Anderson College in Indiana with a major in art, I was hired to create the printed materials for the college and to teach the visual arts class. Not long after that, a college friend of mine, Gary Powell, introduced me to Bill Gaither. This was just a few years after Bill's groundbreaking song "He Touched Me." Pinebrook Studio, now Gaither Studios, was ready to open for business and someone was needed to design record jackets for custom projects. For the next few years my job included designing songbook covers, press kits, and concert information for the Bill Gaither Trio.

By the time Bill started the video series, I had started my own graphic arts business and for years had been away from the realm of gospel music. I was publishing books and freelancing for a large publishing house. My company had published books on lighthouses, little country churches, and bridges — each with an inspirational theme. Drawing faces has always been an interest of mine and it was time for a change.

In August of 2003, I approached my friend, Bill Gaither, about the possibility of drawing about seventy-five singers who had been featured on his video series. My idea was to have a short biographical sketch of each individual across the page from a pen and ink drawing. He gave encouragement to the project. As it turned out, the book has almost doubled in size and I still wasn't able to include all who have been featured. It was hard to leave anyone out but a great deal of effort was made to include the original singers that my dad loved so much.

My dad, Monroe William Liverett, died two months before the first video was recorded in 1991. He would have enjoyed watching every one — he really loved *good music.*

It all started with a song.

David Liverett
Anderson, Indiana

JANUARY 17, 1945 -

# MARY ANN GAITHER ADDISON

*As a founding member of the Bill Gaither Trio, Mary Ann's place in gospel music history is secure.*

In the mid-1950s, a sister and her two brothers—Mary Ann, Danny, and Bill—began singing in small churches and youth rallies in central Indiana. Their concerts consisted of gospel standards perfected around the family piano. When their voices went out on a daily broadcast, sponsored by the grocery store where Bill worked, what came back was a steady stream of invitations to sing not only at churches but also fairs, farm bureau meetings, and civic gatherings. To accommodate their audiences, the trio added some secular favorites to their gospel music concerts. Before long they were singing most evenings and every weekend. That family threesome—Mary Ann, Danny, and Bill—was the genesis of the Bill Gaither Trio.

Eventually, the Trio's tour took them beyond the Indiana borders to nearby states such as Illinois, Ohio, Michigan, Kentucky, and Tennessee. Mary Ann was barely in her teens when the Bill Gaither Trio made its entry into the world of gospel music. Her deep alto voice was the perfect blend with brothers Bill and Danny. Mary Ann sang with the Bill Gaither Trio for eight years.

Married to Don Addison, the mother of two and grandmother of five, Mary Ann today works for the Gaither organization as tour coordinator for Homecoming and Gaither Vocal Band concerts. Like Bill, Mary Ann still lives in Alexandria, Indiana, near Grover's Corners, home of their grandfather, Grover Gaither. In 1999, Mary Ann was inducted with the Bill Gaither Trio into the Gospel Music Association Hall of Fame. As a founding member of the Bill Gaither Trio, she was a pioneer in a field that is still influenced by a style often referred to as, simply, *Gaither music.*

MAY 21, 1923 - JULY 27, 1995

# DORIS AKERS

*Doris' beloved song, "Sweet, Sweet Spirit," has touched the hearts of millions of Christians around the world.*

Tim Spencer, an original member of the Sons of the Pioneers, after becoming a Christian, hearing the music of Doris Akers and the Sky Pilot Choir, Los Angeles, California, signed her to RCA Records and Manna Music Publishing. One Sunday night, before the choir was to march into the evening service, at the world famous Sky Pilot Church, she asked her choir members to pray Heaven down, which she described as a special moment. Doris kept thinking over and over there is a *sweet, sweet spirit* in this place. The next morning she completed what has become a classic gospel song. In 1965, RCA recorded Doris Akers together with the Statesmen Quartet.

In 1993, Doris was invited to a Gaither Homecoming taping. Bill began to play the piano for her to sing her song, "Sweet Jesus." Bill couldn't seem to get the beat the way she wanted it, so she boldly walked over, pushed him off the piano bench, and obviously began to play the beat that only she could play. The Homecoming friends erupted with laughter, especially Bill, who enjoyed that kind of spontaneity which has contributed to the success of the video series.

Doris received numerous awards and in 2001 was inducted into the Gospel Music Association Hall of Fame. Her multiple talents were also honored by the Smithsonian Institute, which labeled her songs and recordings as "National Treasures."

— Judy Spencer Nelon

# Sweet, Sweet Spirit

Doris Akers, 1962

There's a sweet, sweet Spir-it in this place, and I know that it's the Spir-it of the Lord; there are sweet ex-pres-sions on each face, and I know they feel the pres-ence of the Lord.

*Refrain*

Sweet Ho-ly Spir-it, sweet heav-en-ly Dove, stay right here

with us, fill-ing us with your love; and for these bless-ings

we lift our hearts in praise; with-out a doubt we'll know

that we have been re-vived when we shall leave this place.

## Alleluia

Jerry Sinclair, 1972

1. Al-le - lu - ia, al-le - lu - ia, al-le - lu - ia, al-le - lu - ia,

al-le - lu - ia, al-le - lu - ia, al-le - lu - ia, al-le - lu - ia.

2. He's my Savior
3. I will praise Him

JUNE 19, 1934 -

# GLEN ALLRED

*Glen with his smooth baritone voice has been part of the Florida Boys for over forty years.*

G len was born Glennan H. Allred in Monroe, Tennessee, the youngest of the three children of Lola Grace and Homer Allred. While still in grammar school he learned to read music. He remembers "a bunch of cousins who played and I started playing a Gene Autry guitar when I was eight years old. It cost a whopping four dollars." At fourteen, Glen joined the Dixie Drifters, a country band in his hometown of Monterey, Tennessee. The group traveled in a pick-up, all four in the cab. On one of their singing dates they opened a program for Wally Fowler and the Oak Ridge Quartet. Wally asked Glen to go to Louisville the next Sunday to try out for the group. For about a year and a half, in the early 1950s, he played the guitar and sang baritone for the Oak Ridge Boys. After being cut from the group in May of 1952, Glen left Nashville and headed to Valdosta, Georgia, where he joined the Happy Rhythm Quartet. Later that year, he was offered a job with the Gospel Melody Quartet. Soon after that, Les Beasley joined the group and in 1955, they changed their name to the Florida Boys.

Glen has one of the smoothest baritone voices in the business. Besides playing the guitar and singing with style, he is considered to be one of the sweetest and nicest men in southern gospel. Glen has been married to Shirley since 1954. They have two children, Randy and Cindy. He credits Shirley for her strong Christian faith and taking their children to church all those years when he couldn't be there. He says he could not have made it without the support and faith of his family.

Glen was recently inducted into the SGMA Music Hall of Fame and appeared on the February, 2001, cover of *Singing News*.

www.floridaboys.com

**AUGUST 16, 1928 -**

# LES **BEASLEY**

*Les has been a very influential person in the gospel music industry. It was Les who named the Dove Award.*

Les was born Lester George Beasley in Crockett, Texas. As a preacher's kid, Les had plenty of opportunities to sing in church at an early age and loved singing with a group in four-part harmony. Les sang bass in the early groups. A bad case of measles changed his voice forever.

The Beasley family lived in several places in eastern Texas, Louisiana, and Arkansas. When Les moved from West Helena, Arkansas to Beaumont, Texas, he joined the Marines just as the United States entered the Korean War. He saw action in South and North Korea as part of the First Tank Battalion, First Marine Division.

After the war, Les joined the Gospel Melody Quartet in 1955 but soon renamed the group the Florida Boys. He has managed this group for over forty years. He is a lifetime member of the board of directors of the Gospel Music Association and was president for two years. Les is president of The National Quartet Convention which promotes three large events in gospel music: the National Quartet Convention in Louisville, Kentucky, the Great Western Quartet Convention in Sacramento, California, and the Canadian Gospel Quartet Convention in Red Deer, Alberta.

Les was a pioneer in gospel music on television as producer of the nationally syndicated *Gospel Singing Jubilee* program.

A committee of Bill Gaither, Herman Harper, and Les Beasley suggested that the GMA board present an award as part of their annual meeting. It was Les who named it the Dove Award.

Les believes that he is doing what the Lord would have him do and that has kept him singing these fifty plus years.

www.floridaboys.com

19

**MARCH 10, 1959 -**
· · · · · · · · · · · · · · · · · · · · · · · · · · · · · · · · · · · · · · · · · · · · · · · · · · · · · · ·

# ROGER **BENNETT**

*Roger received the Singing News award for Favorite Pianist from
1993 to 2003.*

**P**ianist, vocalist, and songwriter, Roger Douglas Bennett was
born in Jonesboro, Arkansas. At an early age Roger learned to
love southern gospel music and enjoyed the harmonies of the
Florida Boys, the Kingsmen, the Goodmans, and the Cathedrals, the
group he joined in November of 1979. This represented the
fulfillment of a lifelong dream for Roger. To sing southern gospel
music was truly his desire in life. Roger continued with the
legendary Cathedral Quartet until their retirement from the road in
1999. He then helped form one of today's leading quartets, Legacy
Five, with Cathedral baritone, Scott Fowler.

Over the years, Roger has received many awards presented by his
fans and peers, including *Singing News* Favorite Pianist from 1993
to 2003 and the Dove Award for Southern Gospel Song of the
Year in 1999 for "Healing." Roger is also a very accomplished
songwriter, having penned several singles and number one songs.
Roger comments that his favorite song is "Blessed Assurance" and
his favorite self-penned composition is "Whispers in the Night."
Even though the awards were appreciated, the most special and
memorable thing for Roger was the outpouring of love and prayers
when he was diagnosed with leukemia in 1995. "My family and I
literally depended on God everyday to get us through. And God
used our musical family to keep us encouraged. Our lives have been
touched so much by their love and concern." Roger and his wife
Debbie live in Thompsons Station, Tennessee, with their children
Chelsea and Jordan.

— Crystal Burchette

## AUGUST 22, 1911 - OCTOBER 3, 1974

# DOYLE BLACKWOOD

*Doyle, the bass singer of the original Blackwood Brothers, is the father of son, Terry Blackwood, and daughter, Kay.*

Doyle Jimmy Blackwood was born in a three-room shack on a small farm near Ackerman, Mississippi, to sharecroppers, William Emmett and Carrie Blackwood. He had two brothers and a sister. Their family, though poor, was strong and had a deep religious commitment.

Doyle was fascinated by music at an early age. Emmett and Carrie recognized their children's musical talent and sold some valuable prize chickens to finance music lessons. While the older children were at school, Doyle would amuse himself by singing songs he had learned in church that week. He learned to sing harmonies, play the mandolin, and read shaped notes in Sunday School. He commented, "My first and most lasting ambition was to learn everything possible about singing, and then to become a professional gospel singer."

Doyle liked the singing style of the Delmore Brothers and Jimmie Rodgers. His favorite song over the years was "Turn Your Eyes upon Jesus." In the early years of the Blackwood Brothers Quartet, he accompanied the group on the mandolin and guitar. He was also the original manager and master of ceremonies. He was called the "Mighty Mite of the Mike" because he stood all of five feet, three inches and weighed one hundred and two pounds. He always enjoyed a good joke about his size.

Doyle died in 1974 as a result of complications suffered from an accident at his farm in Hernando, Mississippi. His life was one of service to people and obedience to God. Everyone loved him.

Doyle was married to Carmen and their children are Terry and Karen.

— Charles de Witt

www.blackwoodbrothers.com

24

AUGUST 4, 1919 - FEBRUARY 3, 2002

# JAMES **BLACKWOOD**

*James was part of the original Blackwood Brothers and sang second tenor. He is the father of Jimmy and Billy.*

In 1934, fifteen-year-old James Blackwood joined with his brothers, Doyle and Roy, and his nephew, R W to form a group called the Blackwood Brothers. No one could have known then the impact that the Blackwood Brothers and James Blackwood would have on a fledgling style of music known as southern gospel.

It was difficult to make a living in those days and the group disbanded in 1935. At that time, Roy and R W left their hometown of Ackerman, Mississippi. When they returned a couple of years later, the Blackwood Brothers began singing once again.

In 1939, James married Miriam (Mim) Grantham in a double wedding ceremony along with Doyle and his bride, Carmen. Mim became a role model for other quartet wives as she stood by James and realized the calling he had from God.

After World War II ended, the quartet took on a new look with James, R W, and Doyle Blackwood, and Bill Lyles singing bass. It was a group that became famous and made their first television appearance in 1948. 1952 was the year the Blackwood Brothers were considered to have their best quartet yet. James, R W, and Bill were joined by tenor, Bill Shaw. In 1954, they won the *Arthur Godfrey Talent Scouts* program. Not long after, a tragic plane crash in Clanton, Alabama, took the lives of R W Blackwood and Bill Lyles. James said he would never sing again.

After a chance to regroup, Cecil Blackwood became the new baritone, and J. D. Sumner, as bass, rounded out the group.

James was inducted into the GMA and SGMA Halls of Fame and won countless awards and honors for his contributions. He is remembered for singing two songs in particular, "How about Your Heart" and "I'll Meet You in the Morning."

www.blackwoodbrothers.com

# JIMMY BLACKWOOD

*Jimmy is the oldest son of James and Miriam Blackwood. He was healed of pancreatic cancer in 1984.*

It was 1943 and World War II was raging when the Blackwoods moved to National City, California. There on July 31, James and Mim gave birth to their first son, James, Jr. After the war, the family moved back to Iowa where Jimmy began piano lessons at the age of six. In 1950, when they moved to Memphis, Tennessee, James had hopes for Jimmy to play the piano for the Blackwood Brothers Quartet. In 1962, he attended the Stamps School of Music in Dallas, Texas, for more piano instruction and to everyone's surprise he sang his first solo. This began a singing career that has spanned four decades. Jimmy sang with the Junior Blackwood Brothers, and, as a member of the Stamps Quartet and the Blackwood Brothers, was inducted into the GMA Hall of Fame. While Jimmy was with the Blackwood Brothers, they won five Grammys and numerous other nominations. In 2003, Jimmy and the Blackwood Brothers joined the Jordanaires on Englebert Humperdink's first gospel album, also a Grammy nominee.

On a youth fellowship outing, Jimmy met his wife Mona whom he later married in 1963. They have two beautiful daughters and five awesome grandchildren, who surpass any award man has ever given.

In March 1984, Jimmy was diagnosed with pancreatic cancer, with a very short life expectancy, but he was healed. Rev. Dan Betzer wrote the account in the book *Deliverance...In the Valley of Death.*

In 1986, Jimmy began a solo ministry, singing and sharing his testimony of God's miraculous healing power. He continues to bless people in his solo ministry and with the reunion of the Blackwood Brothers Quartet. The Blackwoods were pioneers in the gospel music industry and that legacy continues through the voice of Jimmy Blackwood, whom many say sounds a lot like his famous father.

— Mona Blackwood

www.jimmyblackwood.org

**NOVEMBER 27, 1942 -**

# R.W. BLACKWOOD, JR.

*R.W., Jr. or Winston, as he is also known, has made a career in the music world. His father was one of the original Blackwood Brothers.*

Robert Winston Blackwood, Jr. was born in National City, California, and by the age of eight, his family had moved to Memphis, Tennessee. When Winston was ten, his father heard him singing in the car and told him, "You will be singing in the next Blackwood Brothers concert." It wasn't long after that on June 30, 1954, that his father was killed in a tragic plane crash in Clanton, Alabama.

By the time Winston was twelve, he had sung at a Billy Graham Crusade and also had won the top award on a national television show, the *Ted Mack Amateur Hour*.

As he grew older, Winston was no longer interested in gospel music but wanted to be a rock star, due in part to the influence of Elvis, whom he had known prior to his father's death. After moving to Nashville and not having had much success with his career, he received a call to join with other sons of the original Blackwood Brothers to form the Junior Blackwood Brothers.

Winston had not been in church much after his father's death and had never made a commitment to God. In fact, he had been a "big party boy." As the Junior Blackwood Brothers continued to travel and sing the precious songs his father had sung, his heart became convicted. He gave his heart and life to Jesus Christ at a revival service in 1964.

At present Winston, wife Donna, brother, Ron with his wife, Shelley, and two other men have formed the Blackwood Singers. They perform in Pigeon Forge, Tennessee. Winston's favorite song, "His Hand in Mine," is one that his dad often sang. Married in 1965, Winston and Donna have two children, Andrea and Rob, and seven grandchildren.

www.theblackwoods.com

**OCTOBER 23, 1921 - JUNE 30, 1954**

# RW **BLACKWOOD**, SR.

*In RW Blackwood, Sr.'s name, RW stands for R W— that's why there are no periods after the "R" or the "W."*

**B**orn in Ackerman, Mississippi, RW Blackwood, Sr. and his brother Cecil grew up traveling with their parents, Roy and Susie. Because Roy was an evangelist and church overseer, RW began singing in church and revival services with his father at age three. At eight he was singing tenor in a quartet that his father had formed in the church where he was pastoring. Even then he was a hit. RW was able to attend "singing schools" and "singing conventions" all over the South and Southeast. This schooling, RW's favorite, was where he learned technique, how to read shaped notes, and to perfect his God-given talent. When he would return to the homeplace in Ackerman, Mississippi, he and his uncle, James, two years his senior, would climb a tree and discuss the "singing school" lessons they each had attended.

Beginning in 1934 in Ackerman, the original Blackwood Brothers Quartet, Roy (34), Doyle (24), James (15), and RW (13) traveled in Roy's 1929 Chevrolet. RW soon finished high school there.

RW met and married his wife, Elaine, in Jackson, Mississippi, in 1939. They had two sons, Ron and Winston (R.W., Jr.). While the quartet was working in the Aurora Aircraft Plant in San Diego during World War II, RW was drafted. While serving in Okinawa he formed a quartet. After the war, the Blackwood Brothers bought a plane and R W became the pilot. He was the manager and baritone and was the entity that arranged their RCA Victor recording contract and their appearance on the *Arthur Godfrey Show*.

RW was killed in a plane crash in 1954 in Clanton, Alabama. Jake Hess said that RW was not only "Gospel Music's greatest baritone, but prior to his death, he discussed forming a national quartet convention." It was several years later before dream became a reality.

## OCTOBER 21, 1943 -

# TERRY BLACKWOOD

*Terry is the son of Doyle Blackwood and has created his own distinctive vocal style singing with the Imperials and Andrus, Blackwood & Co.*

Richard Terrell Blackwood was the oldest child of the co-founder of the famous Blackwood Brothers Quartet. He was born in Ackerman, Mississippi, near the Tombigbee National Forest. Terry grew up with one sister, Kay. He feels that the greatest influence in his musical career has been his father. "Dad had this consistent integrity." Although his father, Doyle, had become a music legend, Terry set out to make a way on his own.

Terry, with his own distinctive vocal style, has received acclaim as a trendsetter with the Imperials and Andrus, Blackwood & Company. With his cohorts, Jim Murray, Sherman Andrus, and Armond Morales, he received many Grammy and Dove Awards during the 70s and 80s. The group has recently reunited to live in Hawaii and has released a new CD with the Stamps Quartet called *The Gospel Side of Elvis.* Most of the group members were in the original cast that began with Elvis in 1969 in Las Vegas.

Terry has released a new solo CD, *From the Heart* that features "Shout to the Lord," "So High," and "Somebody's Praying." Many people have been blessed as he has taken this new project to churches across the country. *A Blackwood Homecoming, Volume One* also has continued to sell well to his fans.

Terry and his wife Tina have been blessed with two sons and a daughter, Luke, Jesse, and Leah Carmen-Marie. The doctor had told them that they could never have children!

Today, Terry and his family are living in Hawaii where he has reunited with his friends Jim, Armond, and Sherman to form the Classic Imperials.

www.terryblackwood.com

**OCTOBER 8, 1971 -**

# MICHAEL **BOOTH**

*Michael and his brother, Ronnie, grew up hearing "war stories" from their dad when he sang with the Rebels Quartet.*

The tenor singer with the Booth Brothers, Michael David Booth was born in Tampa and has lived in the state of Florida most of his life. His introduction to music came through hearing "war stories" of his dad's southern gospel group when he sang with the Rebels. Ronnie also listened to southern gospel music while growing up. As a youngster, Michael became interested in playing the drums and would use his mom's pots and pans as a drum set. He continued to play throughout high school, winning state recognition awards, and eventually a jazz scholarship to college.

Singing came late for Michael compared to his brother, Ronnie, who began crooning at the tender age of five. Michael's first attempt to sing came at the age of nineteen. Although he had plenty of confidence playing the drums, singing on stage was a different story. Eventually, however, with lots of practice, his desire to minister through song overcame his fear and started him on the road to becoming a popular singer. Fans not only love his singing, but also his natural talent for making folks laugh. What else would you expect from a guy who wrote a song for his final exam in music theory called "Brown Nose in F Major." By the way, he received an A for the exam!

Michael has had many memorable moments, but the two that stand out are singing with the Cathedrals with George Younce, one of Michael's heroes, and taping a video with Bill Gaither. He says, "God has certainly blessed me with many good things, and the Lord definitely deserves all the glory." Michael lives in Nashville with his wife, Vicki, and their sons Christian and Jonathan.

– Bob Crichton

www.boothbrothers.com

**JUNE 28, 1965 -**

# RONNIE **BOOTH**

*Ronnie co-wrote the song "In His Time" and, as a member of the Booth Brothers, was awarded Male Group of the Year for 2004.*

Fans who hear the Booth Brothers for the first time are impressed with the group's unique sound and the members' warm personalities. Ronald Lee Booth II, Ronnie, the lead singer for the group, is a big reason for the impression. Ronnie was born in Detroit, Michigan, but grew up in Tampa, Florida, when his dad, Ron, Sr., moved the family to join the Rebels Quartet. At the age of five, Ronnie sang *The Night Before Easter* on the Rebel's television program.

As Ronnie went through his teens, his love for music and singing continued to grow. Growing up, he immersed himself in a variety of musical styles from such artists as the Rebels Quartet, the Eagles, Barry Manilow, Nat King Cole, and the Gatlin Brothers. Today, he is able to sing many styles of music with great expertise because of this influence. Ronnie's favorite songs are "I Will Lift My Eyes" by Larry Gatlin and "Love Was in the Room" by Mosie Lister. He has also written one song with Joseph Smith called "In His Time."

The Booth Brothers have been named the 1999 SGMA New Artist of the Year, 2002 SGMA Trio of the Year, and 2004 SGN Male Group of the Year.

Ronnie truly believes God has blessed him with the ability to sing and that this talent should be used to serve the Lord. He feels it is his obligation to do his best to point people to Christ through his singing and testimony. "God has allowed me to live my dream of singing, and I want to do everything I can to encourage the saints and point them to the love of God." Ronnie lives in Plant City, Florida, and has two sons, Ronnie Lee and Daniel.

— Bob Crichton

www.boothbrothers.com

**MARCH 17, 1978 -**

# KELLY CRABB BOWLING

*Kelly sang her first song in church at the age of three and knew in her heart that she wanted to spend her life singing.*

The middle daughter of six siblings, Kelly Layne Crabb, was born in Owensboro, Kentucky. Kelly sang her first song in church at the age of three and knew in her heart that she wanted to spend her life singing. When she was saved as a teenager, Kelly knew that she wanted to sing only Christian music. Kelly's parents were her greatest influences in both singing and listening to Christian music.

Kelly's greatest desire has always been to serve the Lord through music. When the Crabb Family ministry began, this desire was fulfilled. Kelly is featured on several of the Crabb Family's fifteen number one songs including "Don't You Wanna Go," "Trail of Tears," and "Jesus Will Do What You Can't."

Kelly is married to Christian music soloist, Mike Bowling. He has recorded such hits as "Thank God for the Preacher," "The Call," "Take Him Back," and many others.

Kelly and Mike have two daughters, Loryn Hope and Katelanne Elaine. Kelly has been influenced not only by her parents, but also by artists such as the Hoppers, the Isaacs, the Goodmans, the Hinsons, the McGruders, and Michael English. Like her siblings, Kelly has many favorite songs, but most treasured is "Holy Ground." The Isaacs sang this song at the wedding of Kelly and Mike.

"Don't You Wanna Go," featuring Kelly, won the Crabb Family its first Dove Award for Southern Gospel Song of the Year in 2003. "Don't You Wanna Go," was the first single from *A Crabb Collection,* winner of the 2003 Dove Award for Southern Gospel Album of the Year.

— Allison Stinson

www.thecrabbfamily.com

JULY 13, 1965 -

# MIKE BOWLING

*Michael has to his credit four solo recordings, several number one songs, and is noted as one of the most successful soloists in gospel music.*

Michael Lorhen Bowling was born in London, Kentucky. He has a brother and a sister. At a young age, Mike and everyone who knew him sensed a special calling on his life. At nine, Mike began playing piano and singing in church. At fourteen, he began traveling with his aunt and uncle, the Mullins Family, on weekends. When Mike was only sixteen years old, a lifelong dream was fulfilled. He was offered a job with the legendary LeFevres and he moved to Atlanta, Georgia. After a few years, Mike returned home, where he formed a group with his brother and cousins. Mike also completed a degree in respiratory therapy.

In 1995, Mike began singing with the New Hinsons and in October, he joined the Perrys. He was featured on their first number one song, written by Gerald Crabb, "Not Even a Stone." While Mike was with the Perrys, he met his future wife Kelly, of the Crabb Family, at a concert in Boaz, Alabama. Mike and Kelly were married on April 6, 1998, but remained with their respective groups. In 1999, when they learned they were expecting their first child, the time apart was just too much. Mike began his solo career, which has grown beyond his greatest expectations. Mike played piano for the Crabb Family for several years in addition to singing as a soloist at all of their appearances. Mike now travels solely as a solo artist singing on as many of the Crabb Family's dates as possible. Mike is a talented songwriter, writing much of his own material. Mike and Kelly have two daughters Loryn Hope, and Katelanne Elaine. Mike's greatest influences in life are his parents and grandparents. His musical influences include Alphus LeFevre and the late Kenny Hinson. Mike's favorite song is "Please Forgive Me," by Gerald Crabb.

— Allison Stinson

www.mikebowling.net

42

**SEPTEMBER 15, 1970 -**

# JOHN **BOWMAN**

*Married to Rebecca Isaacs Bowman, John sings with the Isaacs and plays guitar and banjo.*

John Bowman grew up in Ararat, Virginia. As the son of Bobby and Diane Bowman, he learned at an early age to play many different instruments. John has a sister, Rachel.

As the husband of Rebecca Isaacs Bowman, John is a current member of the family group, the Isaacs. He is a world-class multi-instrumentalist who has worked and traveled with Alison Krauss and Union Station, as well as, Doyle Lawson and Quicksilver.

As a group, the Isaacs have traveled for over thirty years and are based in Lafollette, Tennessee. Their unique style blends bluegrass harmonies and instrumentation with modern southern gospel lyrics.

The group's musical influences come from all genres of music including bluegrass, rhythm and blues, folk, contemporary acoustic, and southern gospel. They perform frequently at the Grand Ole Opry and are active members of the Gaither Homecoming Video and Concert Series. They travel throughout the year and perform nationally. The Isaacs have been asked to perform the National Anthem for many events, including a Cincinnati Bengals football game, several Nashville Predators hockey games, various political rallies, and recently at Carnegie Hall for a Gaither Homecoming video.

In 1997, John was called into the ministry. When not on tour with the Isaacs, he holds revivals. John and Rebecca have two children, Levi Payton and Jakobi Seren.

John's favorite song is one written by his wife, "Stand Still."

www.theisaacs.com

43

44

AUGUST 2, 1975 -

# Rebecca Isaacs Bowman

*Rebecca Isaacs Bowman is an award-winning songwriter who has made appearances with Dolly Parton, Paul Simon, Mark Lowry, and others.*

As the youngest daughter of the acclaimed family group, the Isaacs, Rebecca Isaacs Bowman, has recorded more than twenty albums and made thousands of live appearances. She is an award-winning songwriter who has made guest appearances as a vocalist with Dolly Parton, Bryan Sutton, Paul Simon, Ralph Stanley, and Mark Lowry. Rebecca was influenced musically by her grandmother Fay Fishman, Tony Rice, James Taylor, the Marshall Family, and Dolly Parton. Songs Rebecca has written include "Stand Still," "Friend to the End," and "He Understood My Tears."

While they are best known as a family act, the individual accomplishments of the Isaacs could have made stars of any of them. In their early days, the children appeared on their parents' regular TV show on a local cable access channel. In 1986, they became a family band, bought a bus, and took their music on the road. At one time, a promoter told the group that they could forget about being accepted in the southern gospel world unless they changed their style. They felt what they were doing was too good and too connected with who they were to change. It was a decision that would prove to make all the difference in the world.

Rebecca married John Bowman on June 4, 1994. They have two children, Levi Payton and Jakobi Seren. Her favorite song is "The Good Shepherd."

www.theisaacs.com

## MAY 19, 1970 -

# JIM BRADY

*Jim joined the Booth Brothers in 2002. He has written over a hundred songs since he was sixteen years old.*

James David Brady, the baritone singer with the Booth Brothers, has a long history of music and singing. He began singing with his mom and dad and seven brothers and sisters when he was five years old. They called themselves the Brady Family, but were affectionately known as the Christian Brady Bunch. He was raised in Houston, Texas, and subsequently moved to Ohio. Jim remembers as a kid always hiding a copy of the *Singing News* in his school books so that he could keep up on the latest gospel music news. This has made him a trivia expert on artists, songs, and writers. When Jim was sixteen, he started writing songs and has since written over a hundred songs. Artists such as Ivan Parker, the Ruppes, and Lordsong have recorded some of his songs.

Jim met his wife, Melissa, at a gospel concert in Atlanta, Georgia. For nine years, Jim sang with the Shulers, who were a trio comprised of Jack Shuler, Melissa Shuler Brady, and Jim. They were best known for their enjoyable mix of traditional and progressive southern gospel. Jim liked to call what they sang "new southern." Melissa is a talented songwriter and singer in her own right. She and Jim have also written many songs together, including an album, *Our Love Songs*, with a bit of "pop" feel.

The main thing that Jim and Melissa want people to know is: "What we do is always and only about the Lord and telling others about Him. When we write and when we sing, it is our desire and our goal, first and foremost, to lift Him up in praise." Jim's favorite song is "He's Been Faithful" by Carol Cymbala. His favorite singer is Melissa, his wife. When they're not traveling on the road, Jim and Melissa live in Nashville, Tennessee.

— Bob Crichton

www.boothbrothers.com

**JUNE 5, 1961 -**

# ANTHONY **BURGER**

*Anthony's piano talent magnifies, honors, and brings glory and adoration to his Lord and Savior, Jesus Christ.*

Anthony Burger is a native of Cleveland, Tennessee. He is a man with much to say, yet he does very little talking. While he is a man of few words, his music speaks volumes. Each time he sits at a piano, he magnifies, honors, and brings glory and adoration to his Lord and Savior, Jesus Christ.

Anthony is the youngest student ever to be accepted into the University of Tennessee's Cadek Conservatory of Music in Chattanooga. He can barely remember a moment when he wasn't playing the piano. Anthony's years at Cadek exposed him to many forms of music, including the classics. However, after dedicating his life to Christ at the age of nine, gospel music became his favorite.

As a teen, Anthony joined the Kingsmen and at seventeen, he was nominated as one of southern gospel music's Top Five Musicians by *Singing News*. He retained the title for ten years. His music has garnered much acclaim resulting in more than fifteen awards and nominations, including Dove Awards, Fan Awards, Diamond Awards and the SGMA's Musician of the Year Award.

In the mid-1990s after setting out on a solo career, Anthony was invited to join the Gaither Vocal Band on the Homecoming Tour. He also regularly travels with Mark Lowry.

Whether he's performing at New York City's Beacon Theater, the White House, the Kennedy Center, a Billy Graham Crusade, a Gaither Homecoming Concert, or traveling across international borders such as Canada, Ireland, Scotland, England, or the Caribbean, Anthony is thankful that God is using his talent to bless and encourage.

Anthony and his wife, LuAnn, have two sons.

www.anthonyburger.com

50

## JUNE 10, 1961 -

# CANDY HEMPHILL
# CHRISTMAS

*As the daughter of LaBreeska and Joel Hemphill, Candy's roots in gospel music go back three generations.*

**B**orn in Bastrop, Louisiana, Candy's roots in gospel music go back three generations. Her grandmother was a member of the Goodman family and her parents, Joel and LaBreeska, met when Joel was playing guitar at a service where LaBreeska and the Goodman family were singing. Named Carmel Lynn but nicknamed soon after her birth, Candy was born just two weeks after her father had taken a pastorate in Bastrop.

In the early 1970s, the family moved to Nashville to explore opportunities in the Christian concert and recording industry. Candy and her brothers, Joey and Trent, were enrolled in correspondence courses and joined their parents on the road. In 1973, when she was only thirteen, Candy's first recording, "I Came on Business for the King," reached fifth place on the gospel music charts.

Candy chose to put her solo career on hold when she met and married Kent Christmas, a dynamic young evangelist. She felt her young family needed a normal and secure life not caught up in the confusion of separate road careers. Daughter Jasmine was born in 1988. In 1994, son Nicholas arrived three months early. He spent nine weeks in the hospital. The young family had no insurance and no income during that time. People they had met all across the country heard the need and sent help. The medical bill of more than three quarters of a million dollars was paid.

Since being invited to participate on the Gaither Homecoming series, Candy's career has taken a new direction. She is recording once again and creating her own songs or collaborating with others.

www.candychristmas.com

**DECEMBER 1, 1959 -**

# KELLY NELON CLARK

*Kelly is the daughter of legendary singer Rex Nelon. In her own right, she has won numerous awards including three Grammy nominations.*

Kelly has been in professional Christian music for twenty-seven years. Touring the world presenting the gospel in song has been her life's calling since the age of thirteen. Her father, Rex Nelon, is a gospel music legend who passed on a legacy of excellence and commitment to the cause of Christ. Her voice has been heard from the small country church to Carnegie Hall and every other venue in between. Kelly continues to set the standard which female vocalists follow. She continues to tour selected dates with her family group, the Nelons, along with her husband and two daughters. Kelly also serves on the staff of their home church in Powder Springs, Georgia.

Kelly's endless pursuit of training and knowledge is represented in every song and every note that she sings. In addition to her work with the Nelons, Kelly has recorded six solo projects. Music fans and her peers have recognized Kelly's hard work, dedication, and talent with three Grammy nominations and six Dove Awards. *Singing News* readers have selected Kelly as Alto of the Year four times, and as Female Artist of the Year four times. The readers of *Voice Magazine* selected Kelly as Female Artist of the Year three times.

"My father took great pride in developing new talent. He was grateful for the opportunities that were given to him when he started, so he never missed the chance to do the same for someone who had talent and possessed a love and desire to perform gospel music — including me," shares Kelly.

— Jason Clark

www.thenelons.com

54

**OCTOBER 11, 1948 -**

# CYNTHIA **CLAWSON**

*Cynthia's most recent recording, "See Me, God," explores the struggles and sorrows of life. It has received overwhelming audience response.*

Cynthia Clawson was born in Houston, Texas, and has been singing the gospel for more than four decades. Called "the most awesome voice in gospel music" by *Billboard Magazine*, she has received a Grammy and five Dove Awards for her work.

Cynthia was three years old when her father first asked her to sing in the small church he pastored. She has not stopped since — from local neighborhood churches to Robert Schuller's *Hour of Power* to London's Wembley Stadium.

A graduate of Howard Payne University with a major in vocal performance and a minor in piano, Cynthia was awarded an honorary degree, doctor of humane letters, from Houston Baptist University in 1995. During her senior year in college, Cynthia was spotted by a CBS television producer who signed her to headline a summer replacement for the *Carol Burnett Show*. That led to a recording contract with Buryl Red. Buryl was writing a musical with friend Ragan Courtney, and Cynthia was invited to record the solos for the original cast album. There Cynthia and Ragan met, were married within six months, and began a lifetime of creative collaboration.

Throughout her career, Cynthia has continued to push beyond the boundaries of traditional gospel music. Her rendition of "Softly and Tenderly" set the evocative tone for the soundtrack of the Academy Award winning movie, *The Trip to Bountiful*.

Currently, Cynthia and Ragan are co-pastors of Tarrytown Baptist Church in Austin, Texas. Son, Will, is pursuing a recording career in Los Angeles and daughter, Lily, is a religious studies major at the University of Texas at Austin.

— Laurie Winton

www.cynthiaclawson.com

**NOVEMBER 27, 1979 -**

# AARON CRABB

*Aaron has written songs that the Crabb Family has recorded such as "Smile Again" and "You Let the Light Back In."*

Born in Owensboro, Kentucky, David Aaron Crabb is the youngest, by only a few minutes, of the six Crabb siblings. His twin brother Adam came into the world before him. Aaron, who sings and plays acoustic guitar with the Crabb Family, actually began his onstage career by playing the bass guitar. Aaron's parents, sister Kelly, and brother Jason had been traveling for several months when Aaron joined them.

Aaron was always very active in sports and enjoyed attending public school. During a summer vacation he traveled with his family to a concert where the Goodmans and Phil Cross & Poet Voices were also on the program. Aaron had developed an interest in playing the bass and in that concert joined the family for the first time. He knew immediately that he had found his place.

After his parents retired from the road, Aaron stepped up to the front line of singing. Aaron has also answered the call to preach and has followed in his father, Gerald Crabb's footsteps as a songwriter. He has written several songs that his family has recorded and has also co-written songs with his brother-in-law, Mike Bowling.

Aaron's greatest influences have been his family and other artists such as Michael English, Russ Taff, and the Gaither Vocal Band. His favorite song is "Through the Fire" written by his father and sung by the Crabb Family at the 2002 Dove Awards program. One of Aaron's career highlights is the Crabb Family's 2003 Grammy nomination. Aaron and his wife Amanda have one son, Elijah David.

— Allison Stinson

www.thecrabbfamily.com

58

**NOVEMBER 27, 1979 -**

# ADAM CRABB

*Adam is a part of the Crabb Family Band, voted by Singing News fans as Band of the Year for 1999, 2001, and 2003.*

As the middle son of the six Crabb children, Adam Lee, was born a few minutes before his twin brother Aaron. Like his twin, the place was Owensboro, Kentucky. Adam sings and plays harmonica with the Crabb Family. He was the last of the six siblings to join the family ministry full time. Although Adam was reluctant, he knew in his heart all along that God had called him. Adam recalls sitting in church one night and feeling God deal with his heart to step out and minister.

Adam's father, Gerald Crabb, is his greatest influence. Gerald, a six-time GMA award-winning songwriter, bought Adam's first harmonica at a Cracker Barrel restaurant. He has also been influenced by some of his favorite singers and musicians such as Michael English and Terry McMillan. Aaron's favorite song is one his father wrote called "The Healer."

Adam is blessed with a God-given talent to play and serves God with one hundred percent of his ability and his heart. He sings much of the group's harmony. The Crabb Family's project, *The Walk*, featuring Adam, was awarded the 2003 Dove Award for Southern Gospel Album of the Year.

Adam has received numerous award nominations for young artists and musicians. He is recognized as one of the most talented musicians in Christian music today.

Adam and his wife Kristi have a daughter, Hannah Grace.

— Allison Stinson

www.thecrabbfamily.com

60

**JANUARY 2, 1958 -**

# GERALD CRABB

*Gerald's award-winning songs have contributed to the success of the Crabb Family.*

Gerald Douglas Crabb was born in the tiny community of Rosine, Kentucky, the only boy in a family of three older sisters, and one younger. As young children, Gerald and his sisters often "played church." Gerald's sisters say that he always landed the role of the preacher. What they did not know was that God had begun an awesome work in the life of a small boy. Gerald's life story consists of playing music, singing, writing songs, preaching, and pastoring.

While pastoring a church in Philpot, Kentucky, Gerald and his wife Kathy felt God leading them to launch a music ministry with their children. Kathy had heard Gerald's songwriting and singing abilities and noticed each of their children developing his or her talents. She knew that it was time to move forward with the ministry of the Crabb Family. In 2002, Gerald and Kathy retired from the road. Both still remain very active in their children's ministry while Gerald focuses more on his personal ministry of preaching, singing, and writing.

Gerald Crabb's story is one of humble, modest beginnings and hardships. Gerald has a powerful testimony of a battle with and deliverance from an alcohol addiction. He has taken the hard knocks in life and turned them into melodies. He has allowed the Lord to transfer times of brokenness and heartache into hope and joy. Gerald has been named GMA's spotlight Songwriter of the Year seven times in the southern gospel division. He also shared BMI's highest honor, Gospel Songwriter of the Year, with Steven Curtis Chapman. The Crabb Family's recording, *The Walk*, featuring songs written by Gerald, was nominated for a Grammy. Although his songs are listed among many of his peer's favorites, one of Gerald's favorite songs was written by James McFall, "I Still Trust You," and is the motto of his life.                                    — Allison Stinson

www.thecrabbfamily.com

**MARCH 3, 1977 -**

# Jason Crabb

*Jason has followed in his father's footsteps both as a singer and as a preacher. As a young child he knew he would be involved in ministry.*

Jason Douglas Crabb was born in Owensboro, Kentucky. As the eldest of six, Jason always looked up to his father, Gerald Crabb, and followed in his footsteps, both as a singer and as a preacher. Even as a young child, Jason knew he would somehow be involved in music and in ministry. He began singing and playing various instruments at an early age. Jason developed his talent by singing and playing in church and was ready to step out into full-time ministry as soon as he felt the calling of God on his life. Jason is featured on many of the Crabb Family hits such as "Please Forgive Me," "Through the Fire," "The Lamb, the Lion, and the King," "Still Holdin' On," " Sure Miss You," "Please Come Down to Me," "That's No Mountain," and "The Cross," all written by his father. Jason helped his father write Mike Bowling's number one hit "Thank God for the Preacher."

Jason and his wife Shellye have a daughter, Ashleigh Taylor. Jason and Gerald co-wrote a song for Ashleigh called "Forever" that has become Jason's favorite song. He also recalls the song, "I Still Trust You," being an encouragement many times in his life. Jason's greatest influence has been his father, as well as Michael English, Russ Taff, the Gaither Vocal Band, and many other artists in Christian music. "The Cross," which features Jason, was awarded the 2003 Dove Award for Southern Gospel Song of the Year. *Singing News* fans named Jason Favorite Young Artist in 2001. He has received numerous other awards and nominations as a male vocalist.

— Allison Stinson

**FEBRUARY 11, 1956 -**

# KATHY CRABB

*The doors that her children have walked through are the direct result of Kathy's hard work and the favor of God.*

Kathy Jo Coppage was born in Centertown, Kentucky. No one knew at that time just what God had in store for the life of this new baby girl. Kathy is the baby of four children (two sisters and a brother). At a very young age, Kathy demonstrated sharp business skills and a strong work ethic. Although the Crabb Family and Gerald Crabb often walk on stages to accept awards or receive honors, Kathy Crabb is often the unmentioned secret to the success of the Crabb Family. Kathy and her husband Gerald have six children: Krystal, Jason, Kelly, Adam, Aaron, and Terah and eight grandchildren. The Lord placed in Kathy's heart the desire to embark upon a music ministry with her children and her husband.

In the days when Gerald pastored a small church in Philpot, Kentucky, Kathy spent countless hours with her children gathered around a piano. She helped each to develop his or her musical and vocal abilities and taught them to sing harmony. Kathy still relies on the direction of God daily to lead her children in their ministry. She has served as a role model to nearly every singer, songwriter, musician, or business person in the southern gospel music industry in some form or fashion at some time.

Kathy believes in hard work and has taught her family the values that she lives. The results are evident through her children's number one songs, Dove Awards, Grammy nomination, and souls saved and lives changed. Kathy's favorite song is one that her husband wrote and her children recorded, "He'll Make a Way."

Kathy's desire is to faithfully and obediently manage her children's ministry and to mentor young singers and musicians who are in love with the music, the message, and most of all, the Lord.

— Allison Stinson

www.thecrabbfamily.com

**AUGUST 17, 1912 - MARCH 21, 1957**

# DENVER CRUMPLER

*While Denver was singing with the Statesmen Quartet, it was considered by some to be the most perfect quartet.*

Denver Dale Crumpler was born in Village, Arkansas, near Magnolia. As a child, Denver sang in churches and at all-day singings near his home. As the radio became the norm in many homes, the public began to hear his wonderful Irish tenor voice. Shreveport, Louisiana, became his home and then Little Rock, Arkansas, where he joined the Stamps-Melody Boys in the mid-1930s. He learned to play the guitar as a young man and would accompany the group. The Rangers Quartet gained respect when Denver joined their group in 1938. For several years, the Rangers made their home in Charlotte, North Carolina, where they worked with a local radio station.

Doy Ott had sung with the Rangers but later joined the Statesmen Quartet. He persuaded Denver to join the group at about the same time the Statesmen became one of the most popular singing groups in the nation. The Statesmen were asked to sing the title song for the movie, *A Man Called Peter*. They later traveled to New York to sing the song for the film's premier. The Statesmen Quartet was declared the winner on the nationally televised *Arthur Godfrey's Talent Scouts* program. This exposure increased their traveling as they toured from Texas to the east coast.

Denver's faith grew stronger during his last days. He settled in Decatur, Georgia, with his family and became very active in his church. Even when he was traveling with the quartets, he would always try to make it back home for church on Sunday.

## MARCH 7 -

# JESSY DIXON

*"There is an element in Jessy's music that can't be mistaken, that element is love...and, wow!, do I feel it!"* — Diana Ross

Jessy Dixon's résumé reads like a Who's Who in gospel music and a worldwide travelogue combined. This man has been "on the move" since his first public performance at age five.

It was not long before he was "discovered" by James Cleveland, who became the first of many gospel greats to record Jessy's compositions. Hundreds of songs and performances later, with folks like Diana Ross, Natalie Cole, Mahalia Jackson, Cher, Bette Midler, James Taylor, and Al Greene, and world tours with Paul Simon, an international smash hit song, "I Am Redeemed," three gold records, and multiple Grammy Award nominations, his friend, gospel music producer, Bob MacKenzie invited him, no, coerced him to a Homecoming recording session at the Gaither studios. Though Jessy knew Gaithers' songs and reputation, he was hesitant about just dropping in on this session where he expected to be out of his comfort zone. What was this crazy MacKenzie man getting him into? Just a huge chunk of the rest of his life! That's all.

Following the break, during which Jessy behaved himself like a good boy, "just sat, smiled, and sang along with the familiar tunes," he returned to the studio and found a handful of the artists singing "Highway to Heaven," just for fun. As the Homecoming group reassembled, Jessy became Jessy! He quietly began to teach the group seated around him a new counter-melody. It caught on, and as more and more singers arrived, it became a real jam session.

Enter Bill Gaither, who is famous for recognizing a great moment, and commanded, "Roll the cameras!" For at least fifteen minutes, this gathering of Homecoming Friends found themselves on an up-tempo journey with a new friend. Jessy had a new family, and Homecoming concerts have never been the same since!

— Joy MacKenzie

www.jessydixon.com

**DECEMBER 20, 1949 -**

# Sue Dodge

*Sue electrifies audiences when during Homecoming concerts she joins members of the Speer Family to sing their hit, "I Shall Never Forget the Day."*

Sue Chenault was born in Little Rock, Arkansas. She can easily trace her gospel roots back to her childhood home and parents who nurtured her love of music. Purchasing a piano for her, early on, they encouraged her to sing. By the age of fourteen, she began her professional singing career with the T. O. Miller Trio.

Not long after she was voted "Miss Congeniality" in the 1968 Miss Arkansas beauty pageant, Sue successfully auditioned with the Downings, a new group in gospel music who immediately became one of its finest. Sue went on to sing soprano for the Speer Family for four years until her marriage to Amos Dodge in 1974.

One of Sue's special memories is performing a patriotic medley prior to a speech by President Reagan. One of the selections, "God Bless the USA" was the president's favorite. Moments after she sang, he opened his remarks by saying, "Politicians are rarely rendered speechless, but you'll have to excuse me. Young lady, that was wonderful."

With a musical career spanning three decades and having won four consecutive Dove Awards for Female Vocalist, Sue is certainly a voice to be reckoned with! She was honored as a former member of the Speer Family when the group was inducted into the GMA Hall of Fame. Sue continues to travel full time sharing in churches, on TV, and singing and speaking at conferences. In addition, she sings, plays the piano, and participates in pastoral ministry with husband Amos in McLean, Virginia.

Daughter Tara with her husband Travis Goodman, grandson of gospel legends, Howard and Vestal, has moved close by. Sue is thrilled to be a full-time grandmother to Sydney.

— Laurie Winton

www.suedodge.com

**JUNE 12, 1945 -**

# ANN DOWNING

*Ann is a Dove Award winner, soloist, and conference speaker.*

Born Virginia Ann Sanders in Pittsboro, Mississippi, Ann Downing grew up on her family's cotton farm dreaming of the day when she would sing gospel music all over the world. Her family made sure she had opportunities to realize that dream, connecting her with the best music teachers and singing schools in the area. Ann listened to a variety of music including Patti Page and Rosemary Clooney, but it was her interest in Ginger Smith Laxson, soprano for the Speers, that really paid off. Right out of high school, Ann was offered a job with the Speer Family, impressing them by knowing all their songs. Ann quickly became one of the most popular vocalists in gospel music with her signature songs, "I Must Tell Jesus" and "On the Sunny Banks."

Within a year of forming the Downings with husband Paul, Ann picked up the Dove Award for Female Vocalist, and three years later was named Queen of Gospel Music by *Singing News*. The Downings changed the face of gospel music with songs such as "Operator," "I've Got Confidence," and "Greater Is He That Is in Me" yet continued to appeal to traditionalists with "Caught Up Together" and "I'll Soon Be Gone." Garnering eighteen Top 20 songs, in a seven-year period, the Downings are notably one of gospel music's legendary groups.

Continuing in full-time ministry since Paul's death in 1992, Ann shares her intensely personal story of a faithful God through great joy and great loss, encouraging others in their journey. Celebrating over forty years in music and ministry, as a member of the Speer Family, the GMA Hall of Famer's top ten hit "Climbing Jacob's Ladder" remains a concert favorite.

— Laurie Winton

www.anndowning.com

**DECEMBER 2, 1932 - FEBRUARY 23, 1992**

# PAUL DOWNING

*Paul reached out to the unloved and hurting people that came his way.*

Paul Shirley Downing, Jr. was born in Manila, Arkansas. The eldest of four children, Paul spent his childhood years in Tupelo, Mississippi, before joining the Navy in 1948. Ever charming, he enjoyed a successful career in sales before finding his home in gospel music. Vocal coach and encourager, Leroy Abernathy, took an interest in Paul's deep bass voice, comparing it to Aycel (A. D.) Sowards, one of the best bass singers from the 1940s. Paul sang with Abernathy's All Stars Quartet, as well as the Rangers Quartet and the Dixie Echoes. He loved Bill Lyles' singing and dreamed of the day he could sing with the Blackwood Brothers.

However, a pretty gal from Mississippi, who was singing with the Speer Family at the time, won his heart and changed those dreams. Paul met and married Ann Sanders in 1968 and within a year, they formed the Downings, becoming one of the most popular groups of the 1970s. Known for introducing many songs to gospel music such as "Rise and Be Healed," "I've Got Confidence," and "Greater Is He That Is in Me," the Downings enjoyed eighteen Top 20 songs in seven years. Paul's unforgettable smile and ability to share his heart in a very special way won the hearts of fans. In 1973, he was awarded the *Singing News* fan award for Favorite Bass.

Through much prayer and healing, Paul and Ann rebuilt their faltering marriage in the late 80s and began reaching out to other couples and hurting kids in need of emotional healing. Paul passed away February 23, 1992, with his dear Ann by his side. It is a little known fact that Paul vocalized the last note on the piano in a vocal lesson shortly before his death. He leaves behind a rich legacy of ministry, sincerely reaching out to the unloved and to hurting people that came his way.

— Laurie Winton

76

## MARCH 18, 1960 -

# JEFF EASTER

*Some of Jeff's best attributes are his ability to love people and to make them laugh. He uses those abilities to encourage others.*

**B**orn Amos Jeffrey Easter, Jeff Easter began playing bass with his family, the Easter Brothers, at the age of eleven. Jeff's daddy was his biggest musical influence. Singing with his family, Jeff developed the bluegrass-tinged voice and country pickin' that he uses today.

Jeff met Sheri Williamson, of the Lewis Family, at an Albert E. Brumley Sundown to Sunup Gospel Singing in Arkansas. He was playing bass for the Singing Americans at the time. Within a year, Jeff and Sheri were married and formed their own successful trio, Jeff & Sheri Easter. The group has given new meaning to the southern gospel music world as they have added their distinct touch of country-driven melodies and down-home charm to the Gospel message. Sheri's raspy, award-winning vocals have combined with Jeff's musicianship, bluegrass-oriented vocals, and stage antics to create a winning combination.

After two Dove Award wins, multiple nominations, and Gaither Homecoming concert tours and videos, Jeff & Sheri Easter's message remains focused on the Gospel message and songs about life and love in our everyday world. They are also known for their uplifting songs about the relationship between a wife and husband and the importance of love and family.

Jeff and Sheri reside in Lincolnton, Georgia, with their two children, Madison and Morgan. Jeff describes himself as "the typical preacher's kid" and affirms that all the bad things one hears about preachers' kids are true! For Jeff, his teenage years were filled with bad choices that led to discouragement. He feels that his ministry in Christian music is one of encouragement.

— Celeste Winstead

www.jeffandsherieaster.com

# SHERI EASTER

*Sheri considers her ministry to be one of compassion and empathy and to encourage people who are hurting.*

Sheri Easter, born Sheri Lynn Williamson, began singing with her family, the legendary Lewis Family, at the age of fifteen. Her mother, Polly Lewis Copsey, who has been her biggest musical influence, has a soulful sound that Sheri loves.

Sheri married Jeff Easter, known previously for his singing and musicianship with the Easter Brothers; and not long afterward, the two formed their own family group that has been traveling for over fifteen years. Jeff & Sheri Easter are known for such hits as "Roses Will Bloom Again," "Thread of Hope," "Praise His Name" and many others. Sheri has been named Female Vocalist of the Year four times and Alto of the Year eight times. The group has received a Grammy nomination and two Dove Awards for Country Album of the Year and Country Recorded Song of the Year. The group is known for its unique country, bluegrass, gospel style and for singing not only gospel songs about heaven but also songs about everyday life and love.

Making their home in Lincolnton, Georgia, Jeff and Sheri have two children, Madison and Morgan, who now travel and perform with the group. Sheri stays busy as a wife, mother, and group business manager. She also enjoys managing her clothing boutique, The Easter Parade, as well as writing songs.

Growing up, Sheri's family was always a close one; so when her father passed away suddenly from a heart attack when she was twenty, it was devastating to her life. Perhaps that has been an influence on her calling to minister through music as she states, "My ministry is one of compassion and empathy and to encourage people who are hurting."

— Celeste Winstead

www.jeffandsherieaster.com

**APRIL 12, 1962 -**

# MICHAEL ENGLISH

*Michael was a member of the Gaither Vocal Band from 1984 until 1991. In 1992, his first solo album was released.*

**B**orn in North Carolina, Michael was reared in a strict, religious family. He was still in grade school when he began singing with his family's group, the Singing Samaritans. In 1980, he joined the Singing Americans and then sang with the Happy Goodman Family's troupe. Michael joined the Couriers for a short time and then returned to sing with the Singing Americans for a year. His big break came when Bill Gaither invited him to join the Gaither Vocal Band in 1984.

Michael's first solo album which was released in 1992 included landmark songs, "In Christ Alone," "Mary, Did You Know?," "Solid As the Rock," and "Heaven." His next album the following year was called *Hope* and included "Message of Mercy," "Love Moves in Mysterious Ways," and "Holding Out Hope to You."

In 1995, Michael released a pop album with Wynonna. In 1996, "Your Love Amazes Me" from his pop album *Freedom* became a top ten hit on Adult-Contemporary charts. Three years later, he returned to his roots with an album simply called *Gospel.*

The next major release, *Heaven to Earth,* was in 2000. While premiering it on the Trinity Broadcast Network, Michael gave his testimony about how God had helped him through the pain in his life, his struggle with addiction to painkillers and his rehab experiences.

In 2002, Michael married Marcie Staambaugh. They have a daughter named Isabella Grace. Michael has a daughter, Megan Leigh Ann English, from a previous marriage. She has a beautiful voice and occasionally sings with her dad.

Michael has reconnected with his old friends, Mark Lowry and Reggie Smith, and they are considering a project together.

www.michaelenglish.org

## NOVEMBER 10, 1947 -

# LARRY FORD

*Larry's passion for ministry abroad has led to his being described as "gospel music's ambassador to the world."*

Larry Don Ford is originally from Lubbock, Texas. His music ministry has taken him to forty-eight of the fifty states in the United States. Larry's facility with language has made it possible for him to carry the message of Christ to twenty-seven foreign countries. From the sounds of grand opera to the stages of southern gospel, Larry has found audiences responding to his commanding voice and anointed ministry.

Larry began traveling and singing across Texas when he was sixteen. Lou Wills Hildreth produced Larry's first recording that same year. He left music for a couple of years but returned as a featured soloist with Paul and Ann Downing's group. In 1980, he became a part of the James Blackwood Quartet, singing tenor on a temporary basis.

Larry's early gospel music influences were James Blackwood, his beloved friend and mentor, and the Blackwood Quartet, as well as the Couriers and the Imperials. Among classical musicians, he loved listening to Placido Domingo and Jussi Bjoerling. Today, Larry's favorite classical tenor is his brother, Bruce.

In February, 2003, Larry was awarded a Grammy for Best Southern Gospel Recording. The project that won the award was *They Called Him Mr. Gospel Music: A Tribute to James Blackwood.* Larry participated in Bill and Gloria Gaither's Grammy Award winner, *Homecoming at the Kennedy Center* in 2000. He has been a featured soloist on many of the Gaither Homecoming videos.

Larry and his wife Sherryl have been married for thirty-four years. They have four sons, one daughter, and four grandchildren.

www.larryford.com

**JULY 9, 1966 -**

# SCOTT FOWLER

*Scott, the lead singer with Legacy Five, was honored with the Southern Gospel Music Guild's Humanitarian Award in 2004.*

Having been a fan of quartet music since the age of sixteen, Scott was asked in 1991 to join his favorite group, the Cathedrals. He quickly became one of the most popular baritones in the field of southern gospel music. His dynamic voice and winning personality have made him a favorite.

Scott says the greatest influences on his life and ministry were his dad and Grandpa Hamm. He also stated, "Both men were great preachers, but beyond that they were mentors and heroes. All of my favorite memories seem to have both of these men present. They are in heaven today, but the contributions they left me and my life will remain here forever." Scott's earliest memories are of singing in church. His favorite song is "Wonderful Grace of Jesus."

In 1999, the Cathedrals Quartet said farewell and Scott, along with Roger Bennett, formed one of today's most popular quartets, Legacy Five. Scott now sings lead for the fan favorite while Glenn Dustin, Frank Seamans, and Scott Howard complete the other three parts. Roger Bennett rounds out the group on piano and occasionally sings.

In 2004, Scott was honored with the SGMG Humanitarian Award for his efforts during friend and Legacy Five co-founder Roger Bennett's battle with cancer. Scott was the driving force behind raising the money for Roger's bone marrow transplant, as well as other expenses accrued during his illness.

Scott Fowler is married to Taryn Davis, daughter of Christian comedian, Ken Davis. "Taryn grew up in a home where the husband traveled on weekends, so she was accustomed to the lifestyle." They have a son, Preston, and live in Franklin, Tennessee.

— Crystal Burchette

www.legacyfive.com

**MARCH 28, 1936 -**
. . . . . . . . . . . . . . . . . . . . . . . . . . . . . . . . . . . . . . . . . . . . . . . .

# BILL GAITHER

*And he still directs the choir.*

Just out of college and teaching high school English, Bill Gaither took on a part-time job as choir director at his home church. That's when he first wondered if there just might be a void in the church for songs that combined good theology and the stories of everyday struggles. As history would show, Bill and a co-writer, wife Gloria, would fill that void with nearly 700 songs, pioneering a new genre, often referred to as "Inspirational." In many ways, as much as he is a concert artist, songwriter, video producer, mentor, and entrepreneur, Bill Gaither is still, in his heart of hearts, a choir director. And for the last decade, he's had the opportunity to direct some of the top voices in the country as they've traversed the world—including stops in Ireland, England, Australia, and Israel—as the Homecoming Friends. With these same "Friends," he has produced a succession of nearly 100 videos, a catalog of videos that gave new life to southern gospel music and its living legends as the 20th century came to a close. In the first years of the 21st century, Bill continues to release videos that top the *Billboard* video charts, proving that even mainstream audiences are interested in American music that has a message. Appearing on the Homecoming stage each night is Bill's Gaither Vocal Band, a group that redefined the term "quartet," when it was born in 1981, and one of the first Christian groups to sell out concerts in auditoriums and arenas. Across his 30-plus years, Bill has gratefully accepted five Grammy Awards and nearly thirty Dove Awards. In 1983, he was inducted into the Gospel Music Association Hall of Fame and in 2000 was honored by the American Society of Composers, Artists, and Publishers as "Christian Songwriter of the Century."

— Jack Williams

www.gaithernet.com

# He Touched Me

William J. Gaither

1 Shack - led by a heav - y bur - den, 'Neath a load of
2 Since I met this bless - ed Sav - ior, Since He cleansed and

1 guilt and shame— Then the hand of Je - sus touched me,
2 made me whole, I will nev - er cease to praise Him—

1 And now I am no long - er the same. He touched me, O He
2 I'll shout it while e - ter - ni - ty rolls.

touched me, And O the joy that floods my soul; Some-thing

hap-pened, and now I know, He touched me and made me whole.

# Because He Lives

Gloria Gaither
William J. Gaither

1 God sent His Son, they called Him Je - sus, He came to love,
2 How sweet to hold a new-born ba - by, And feel the pride
3 And then one day I'll cross the riv - er, I'll fight life's fi -

1 heal, and for - give; He lived and died to buy my
2 and joy He gives; But great - er still the calm as -
3 nal war with pain; And then as death gives way to

1 par - don, An emp - ty grave is there to prove my Sav - ior lives.
2 sur - ance, This child can face un - cer - tain days be - cause He lives.
3 vic - tory, I'll see the lights of glo - ry and I'll know He reigns.

Be - cause He lives I can face to - mor - row, Be - cause He lives

all fear is gone; Be - cause I know He holds the

fu - ture, And life is worth the liv - ing just be - cause He lives.

**NOVEMBER 20, 1938 - APRIL 6, 2001**

# DANNY GAITHER

*As part of the original Bill Gaither Trio, Danny received Grammy and Dove Awards for his outstanding voice.*

D aniel Joseph Gaither was born and reared in Alexandria, Indiana. He was the second son of George and Lela Gaither. His foundational role with the Bill Gaither Trio, along with older brother Bill and younger sister Mary Ann, endeared him to audiences around the world. Perhaps he is best remembered, by the ones who knew him well, for the person he was when he was not on stage, when no one was watching. His timeless, heartfelt vocals propelled the Gaither Trio to critical acclaim, countless awards, and sellout concerts across America.

After Danny graduated from Ball State University, he sang second tenor with the Golden Keys Quartet for about five years. Other members included Jim Hill, Pat Duncan, Clarence Claxon, with Harold Patrick on the piano. Jim Hill remembers that Danny was always smiling and that people loved him. Years later, Jim was invited to sing a song that he had written, "What a Day That Will Be," at Danny's funeral.

Dan was a high school teacher, a solo recording artist, and the Minister of Music at Chesterfield Community Church in Chesterfield, Indiana. In 1999, as a member of the Bill Gaither Trio, he was inducted into the Gospel Music Association Hall of Fame.

A touching public moment occurred during Danny's illness. He was in the audience at a Praise Gathering event. Mark Lowry surprised Danny by bringing the microphone to him while they were singing "Something Beautiful." Danny sang a verse and the heavens opened up.

Though a lengthy, courageous battle with illness cut his life short, Danny will be long remembered by his family, friends, and fans for his humanitarian spirit, incredible talent, Christian love, and winning smile.

Danny's favorite song was "Oh Love That Will Not Let Me Go." He "Traced the rainbow through the rain," and believed that "Life shall endless be."                — Vonnie Gaither Wright

**MARCH 4, 1942 -**
· · · · · · · · · · · · · · · · · · · · · · · · · · · · · · · · · · · · · · · · · · · · · · · ·
# GLORIA GAITHER

*The songwriter heard 'round the world.*

A student of French, English and sociology in college, Gloria Sickal wasn't planning on a career in music. Then she met a determined young songwriter named Bill Gaither. In Bill she found a soul mate who understood her passion for eternal themes beautifully told. Those themes would eventually grace nearly 700 Gaither songs, many of which appear in church hymnals around the world. Although Gloria performed with the Bill Gaither Trio for twenty years, is heard on sixty Gaither recordings, and can be seen today on music videos with the Homecoming Friends, music is only part of her calling as a communicator. She has written a shelf of books that include *Making Ordinary Days Extraordinary, Creating Family Traditions,* and *What My Parents Did Right,* among others, plus a series of children's books. She has taught songwriting at the university level, is an active advocate for Christian higher education, earned a master of arts degree in English literature, and has received numerous honorary degrees. A true bibliophile, Gloria shares her reading recommendations in "Gloria's Book Club," a feature found in each issue of *Homecoming Magazine.* In recent years, she has researched the life and works of American author John Steinbeck. A popular speaker on issues that impact today's Christian, Gloria keeps a keen eye on contemporary culture. In 2000, Gloria was recognized by the American Society of Composers, Artists, and Publishers as "Christian Songwriter of the Century" for her musical impact on American culture. But Gloria keeps her accomplishments and commitments in context. Her first priority has always been the making of magical memories for her busy family and encouraging others to do the same for their families.

— Jack Williams

www.gaithernet.com

**DECEMBER 8, 1951 -**

# JOY GARDNER

*Joy learned early that music can make an eternal difference in the lives of people.*

J oy Dyson was born in Little Rock, Arkansas, into a musical family that considered ministry a priority and embedded in Joy's heart the belief that music can make an eternal difference in the lives of people. Growing up and traveling to all-night singings to hear the Statesmen, the Blackwood Brothers, and the Speer Family fueled her appreciation of gospel music and in 1970, Joy successfully auditioned for a spot with the Downings, one of the most popular groups of that decade. Remaining with the group for seven years, she won the Dove Award for Female Vocalist in 1976.

During the 70s and 80s, Joy worked as a studio singer, performing weekly on the Grand Ole Opry and sang with many gospel and country artists such as Dolly Parton, Porter Waggoner, Sandi Patty, Larnelle Harris, and Michael W. Smith. She continues to serve as a background vocalist on various artists' recordings and remains a part of Parton's backup group, performing most recently on the *David Letterman Show* and the *Today Show*.

Joy's involvement with the Gaither Homecoming videos and concerts is a rebirth of sorts, reminiscent of her days of singing alongside her friends and long-time heroes. Convinced that sharing the gospel in song can bring encouragement, hope, and healing like nothing else, Joy continues to share her gift of communicating the message of a song with the Homecoming crowds, as well as sharing her writing, arranging, and directing abilities with her home church.

Together with husband Landy Gardner, Joy leads the internationally recognized Christ Church Choir in Nashville. She has two daughters, Dionne, and Lauren. Her favorite hobby these days is playing grandmother to Dionne's son, Dyson Scott.

— Laurie Winton

**MAY 2, 1948 -**

# LARRY GATLIN

*Larry has enjoyed a phenomenal career in country music, but his heart has always been in gospel music.*

Larry Wayne Gatlin was born in Seminole, Texas. He began performing gospel songs with his younger brothers for a radio station in Abilene, Texas, at age seven. As lead singer and songwriter for the Gatlin brothers, Larry has enjoyed a phenomenal country music career spanning more than twenty-five years, but his heart has always been in gospel music. With Number One country music hits written by Larry and multiple Grammy Awards, the Gatlins are a household name in country music.

When Bill Gaither gathered the first little band of Homecoming Friends in a Nashville recording studio a few years ago, Larry Gatlin was there stirring up the excitement, singing with his gospel heroes. Later, *The Gatlin Brothers Come Home,* produced by Bill Gaither, became a best seller in the Gaither Hall of Honor series.

In the 90s, Larry starred in the Broadway hit, *The Will Rogers Follies.* He followed that by headlining a major theatrical production, *Civil War.* His life story, *All the Gold in California,* named for one of Larry's hit songs, was released by Thomas Nelson Publishers in 1998.

When this famous country star shows up at a Gaither video taping with his Homecoming Friends, everyone in the studio listens in quiet awe at the vocal beauty and depth of expression of Larry Gatlin. These moments make me glad that years ago in Texas, we made the Gatlins' first recordings on Sword & Shield Records, owned by the Wills Family. Larry was inducted into the Texas Gospel Music Hall of Fame in 1997.

Currently Larry and the Gatlin Brothers are performing selected "Reunion Concerts" in Branson, Missouri.

— Lou Wills Hildreth

www.gatlinbrothers.com

**MARCH 12, 1960 -**

# KAREN PECK GOOCH

*She has been honored as Favorite Soprano eleven years consecutively and awarded Female Vocalist of the Year three times.*

**B**orn in Gainesville, Georgia, Karen Peck Gooch has redefined the word "soprano" in the southern gospel music industry. Karen attended Brenau College as an education major with a minor in music. She began her career in 1980 with Alphus LeFevre's group and continued with the Nelons for ten years before starting Karen Peck & New River in 1991. Karen has two sisters, Sandra Peck and Susan Peck Jackson. Susan performs with Karen in New River.

The group is known for such hits as "Four Days Late," awarded Song of the Year twice in 2001, and many more. Many of the songs for which they are known were written or co-written by Karen.

Karen says that one of her greatest honors was traveling with Rex Nelon. His aim was not getting standing ovations. He was more concerned with making sure the music was quality and that each one gave one hundred percent.

Karen's other musical influences include her mother, Sue, and her piano teacher, Eliza Feldman. She enjoys vocalists ranging from Janet Paschal and Céline Dion to Alison Krauss and Sandi Patty. Her favorite song is "Amazing Grace," and she has experienced that grace in her own life. Karen explains, "Saved at eight years old, as a small child, God placed in my heart the desire to sing gospel music. I am very thankful to the Lord for giving me the desires of my heart. I am very blessed to travel with my husband, Rickey, and my children along with my sister Susan and her family. I am living my dream."

Karen and Rickey have two children, Matthew and Kari. Rickey is the sound technician and manager for Karen Peck and New River. The Gooch family resides in Dahlonega, Georgia.

— Celeste Winstead

www.karenpeckandnewriver.com

**NOVEMBER 7, 1921 - NOVEMBER 30, 2002**

# HOWARD **GOODMAN**

*What mattered most to Howard "Happy" was his family.*

Bill Gaither has referred to Howard and Vestal Goodman as "National Treasures." They celebrated fifty-three years of marriage that began after singing in Nashville at the Ryman. After that concert, they drove to Tupelo, Mississippi, where they were married. The original Happy Goodman Family was founded by Howard, also lovingly known as "Happy," and began singing in the 1940s. Howard taught his seven brothers and sisters, Gussy Mae, Stella, Eloise, Ruth, Sam, Rusty, and Bobby to sing and play instruments. Rusty often remarked, "When Howard married Vestal Freeman, it was the smartest thing he ever did." With Rusty and Sam, they became a quartet that was awarded the first Grammy for a gospel group. The list of awards was long but what really mattered to Howard was his family, wife, Vestal, son, Rick (Dianne), and daughter, Vickie (Clark), four grandchildren, three great-granddaughters, and a large extended family.

Howard also pastored a church in Madisonville, Kentucky, and insisted that the group be back home in time for church most Sundays. Howard played the piano and wrote hits including "Give Up" and "I Don't Regret a Mile."

At video tapings, Bill Gaither would ask Howard to entertain, as only he could, by playing "Telling My Blues Good-bye." He laughed and said, "People enjoyed watching him play the piano more than listening." Most of us agree, watching and listening to Howard was a pleasure. Thirteen months before Vestal joined the love of her life in heaven, she said, "When on stage with the Homecoming Friends, I reached over to hold the hand next to me and it wasn't Howard's. I felt like the loneliest person in the world." She had carried on, as his last wish for the woman he loved was, "Sing, Baby, sing." In heaven they sing together.

— Judy Spencer Nelon

www.vestalandfriends.com

**SEPTEMBER 2, 1932 - NOVEMBER 11, 1990**

# RUSTY GOODMAN

*Rusty was a celebrated songwriter of songs such as "I Wouldn't Take Nothing for My Journey Now," and "Who Am I?"*

Charles Frances "Rusty" Goodman was born into a family of eight children in Cullman, Alabama. Rusty had a great ear for harmonies and was a driving force in creating the "Goodman sound." Most of the music recorded by the Goodmans was written by Rusty.

In 1958, Rusty married Billie Dumas. Their daughters are Tanya and April. They have two granddaughters, Mallory and Aly Sykes. Rusty's favorite songs were "The Love of God" and "In the Garden." His favorite singer was Frank Sinatra. Rusty was nominated for and received numerous awards in his lifetime, including Dove and Grammy Awards. He was inducted into the GMA Hall of Fame, both as an artist and as a member of the Happy Goodman Family.

Daughter Tanya remembers, "When we lived in Kentucky, the Goodman Family had a recording studio. My dad would often surprise my mom by bringing extras home for dinner, and I don't mean one or two. It wasn't unusual for him to bring home six, eight, or ten people. Mom was always gracious and whipped up something wonderful to eat, and we'd sit around and laugh and listen to them tell their "road stories." Occasionally, Dad would get out the ice cream freezer and make a batch of his homemade ice cream. He loved to have a house full of company, especially around the dinner table."

Tanya tells a story Rusty told about listening to the Grand Ole Opry. "He liked to put his radio, tuned to WSM, in the window, then go outside and lie on the ground between his house and the neighbor's, also with a radio tuned to WSM, and listen, surrounded by sound. He was a pioneer of stereo and didn't even know it."

— Tanya Goodman Sykes

103

**MARCH 19, 1931 - AUGUST 5, 1991**

# SAM GOODMAN

*Sam was best known for his impromptu humor that came straight from his witty brain. He was one of gospel music's original funny men.*

**B**orn in Bremen, Alabama, Sam was one of the eight children of Drew Sam and Gussie Mae Goodman. Since Howard began traveling as an evangelist at a young age, all the siblings were recruited from the 1930s to the 1950s to sing. Various brothers and sisters made up the Happy Goodman Family. Over the years some would leave to get married or join the military.

In 1957, after serving in the Air Force, Sam met Barbara Gibson at a tent meeting in Earlington, Kentucky, where the Goodmans were singing. They were married in 1957 and had sons Drew Todd and Sam Kristin. In the early 1960s, Howard, Vestal, Sam, and Rusty moved to Madisonville, Kentucky, and founded Life Temple Church. They continued to sing in concerts through the week, then rushed home for church on Sunday morning.

Sam became known as the comic and spokesperson. He would introduce the members of the group and the songs on albums and would include recitations such as "The Goodman Family Story," "Beauty of the Child," "and The Pledge of Allegiance." He would also tell humorous stories on stage. Sam sang with the Goodman Family up into the 1980s. In 1982, he received ministerial credentials. In 1990, he reunited with Howard, Vestal, and Rusty to record what would be their final album, *The Reunion*, which received a Grammy nomination that year. Sam continued to travel, preaching and singing, until his death in 1991.

Through the decades, the Happy Goodman Family received many Grammy nominations, two Grammy Awards and sang at the White House for President Carter. In 1998, they were honored to be inducted into the GMA Hall of Fame.

— Kris Goodman

**DECEMBER 13, 1929 - DECEMBER 27, 2003**

# VESTAL GOODMAN

*Beloved and celebrated, Vestal was inducted into the GMA Hall of Fame and SGMA Hall of Fame.*

The name Vestal Goodman conjures up so many images...images of a waving white handkerchief, big hair, an even bigger smile, mischievous eyes, contagious enthusiasm for life and family and friends, a strong voice, and an even stronger faith. If Vestal Goodman was in your corner, you had God and Jesus and all the angels on your side, and maybe even a coconut cake in your refrigerator.

I remember an artist get-together during GMA week sometime in the mid-80s. All of us were sort of wandering around the circle of folding chairs, trying to fit in, or stand out, or whatever you do when you want to feel like you belong to your group of co-workers (especially when the communication lines are a little rusty or unfamiliar). Vestal walked through the door and into that circle like the queen of the Macy's Day Parade and lost no time gathering all of us under her wing. She laughed and listened, shared road stories, and somehow during our time together made all of us feel more important to God's work and more valuable to his kingdom than any of us had felt when we walked into that room.

In this day and age when youth is idolized and the aged are undervalued to the point of becoming invisible, Vestal carved a broader path and made a deeper impression on us all, the longer she lived.

When I think of her, I'm reminded of those words of Frederick Buechner: "When you remember me, it means that you carried something of who I am with you...It means that even after I die, you can still see my face and hear my voice and speak to me in your heart." Vestal, we remember you. Your voice, your smile, your faith. Your family, your handkerchief, your love...until we meet again.

— Amy Grant

www.vestalandfriends.com

**OCTOBER 30, 1953 -**

# BUDDY GREENE

*Buddy is a virtuoso on the harmonica and with Mark Lowry wrote the Dove Award nominated song, "Mary, Did You Know?"*

Born Lee Rufus Greene in Macon, Georgia, Buddy Greene spent his growing up years learning songs on the ukulele and later moved on to the acoustic guitar. He immersed himself in popular music styles of the time such as Elvis, the Beatles, and Motown. Buddy developed a keen interest in the history of country, bluegrass, and rhythm and blues that is reflected in his music today.

Not only is Buddy a world-class virtuoso on the harmonica, but he is also an exceptional guitarist, songwriter, and singer. His 1990 album, *Sojourner's Song,* brought his music to a wider, national audience when it won the 1991 Dove Award for Best Country Album. In 1992, with Mark Lowry, Buddy co-wrote "Mary, Did You Know?" The song earned him another Dove nomination and has become a Christmas standard. It has been recorded by Kenny Rogers, Kathleen Battle, Natalie Cole, Reba McEntire, Gary Chapman, and many others.

In a recent project, *Rufus*, Buddy revisits his formative years, as he combines bluegrass, blues, and the Beatles into a celebration of acoustic music. As Buddy says, "It's just me having fun with some really talented friends, playing a bunch of old and new songs I like to play, and remembering why I ever wanted to be a musician in the first place." If a recent concert to a packed house in Nashville is any indication, *Rufus* will be a superb addition to Buddy's body of work.

Buddy and his wife, Vicki, live in Brentwood, Tennessee. They have two daughters, Erin and Georganna.

www.buddygreene.com

**DECEMBER 16, 1966 -**

# RODNEY GRIFFIN

*Rodney is a member of Greater Vision and has been presented Songwriter of the Year at the Singing News Fan Awards for six years.*

There is no denying that a Rodney Griffin song has in some way touched everyone who enjoys southern gospel music. From "My Name Is Lazarus" to "Faces," his lyrics and music combine to create moments that take you back to a loved one, a memory, a God that is real, and on and on. But it was when Rodney's parents took him to such concerts as the Downings, the Happy Goodmans, and the Cathedrals, that Rodney developed his love for gospel music at an early age and built the foundation for not only his songwriting, but also his vocal ability. Rodney Paul Griffin was born in Newport News, Virginia. He was saved at age twelve. "The preacher gave the invitation that night. I knew I was lost. I came forward, took his hand, and we prayed. It was a special night for our family...the preacher was my dad, Jeff Griffin."

Before Rodney ever picked up a pen to write a gospel song, he sang in high school with three other guys from the Fellowship of Christian Athletes, called Fellowship Qt. "After college, I moved back to where I was born and worked at Newport News Shipbuilding. I started writing songs at my desk. However, I wanted to sing. I joined a local group called the Galileans. I wanted to sing more. I went full-time in 1991 and joined the Brashears out of Russellville, Arkansas. That fall, I met the Dixie Melody Boys at the National Quartet Convention in Nashville, and joined them soon after. After two years, I joined Greater Vision."

Rodney admits, "I guess my favorite song I've written is either 'I've Been There' or 'The Spirit of Brokenness.' Both continue to speak to me when I hear them." He and his wife, Regina, have two daughters, Reagan and Riley.

— Crystal Burchette

www.greatervisionmusic.com

**DECEMBER 12, 1964 -**

# ERNIE **HAASE**

*Ernie joined his "dream" quartet, the Cathedrals, in 1990. After they retired, he became a founding member of Signature Sound.*

**B**orn in Evansville, Indiana, Raymond Ernest "Ernie" Haase III began his professional singing career in 1986 at the age of twenty-one when he joined the gospel group, Redeemed, headed by singer and songwriter, Squire Parsons. They toured extensively throughout the United States and Canada, and it was then that Ernie realized his calling as a full-time traveling evangelist, singing and proclaiming the Good News.

In 1990, Ernie joined the Cathedrals, his dream quartet and southern gospel's most elite and prestigious. Ernie didn't marry the boss's daughter to get the job. He had joined the group before he met bass singer George Younce's daughter, Lisa. Ernie says that "lightning flashed and thunder rolled." Eight months, later they were married.

Singing tenor with the Cathedrals placed Ernie on thousands of stages around the country and gave him a special place in the hearts of gospel music followers. He is a role model for the young and a torchbearer of traditional gospel music to the aged.

When the Cathedrals retired in 1999, Ernie did full-time solo work, but it wasn't long before he was called to be a part of Old Friends Quartet. Today, Ernie sings with the group, Signature Sound Quartet, that he and George co-founded. The group is a big hit with "What a Savior" and "Stand by Me."

Ernie has appeared on numerous television and radio programs and is a regular on the Gaither Homecoming videos. He has received the Favorite Tenor and Horizon Awards from *Singing News*. With the Cathedrals and Old Friends Quartets, he has been nominated for several Dove Awards. Ernie and Lisa make their home in Stow, Ohio.

www.erniesigsound.com

114

# DECEMBER 30, 1970 -
··············································································

# MARSHALL HALL

*Marshall is the newest member of the Gaither Vocal Band. His songs have appeared on several Homecoming videos.*

**B**orn in Lexington, Kentucky, Marshall Kip Hall grew up singing along with his favorite Kenny Loggins and Kool & the Gang records, but it wasn't until high school that he began to view music as more than a hobby. At sixteen, he attended the Kentucky Governor's School for the Arts and was inspired to follow music as his career path.

Marshall got his chance while attending college at his father's alma mater, Anderson University. During his internship at a local church, a producer approached him to sing for the famed Gaither Studios. Marshall was hooked. He soon began singing for national clients such as McDonald's, Disney, and Warner Brothers, and for artists such as Sandi Patty, Carman, and Clay Crosse. Later, Marshall looked to friend Benjamin Gaither to find a new creative outlet that would employ both his music and his heart for ministry — songwriting. His songs have appeared on records for Salvador, David Phelps, Point of Grace, and several Gaither Homecoming videos, including *God Bless America*, where he and Benjamin performed "Carry Us On," a tribute to the victims of 9/11.

In late 2001, Marshall's ministry took yet another turn when Mountain Park Community Church in Phoenix, Arizona, invited him to be a guest worship leader. There, he found a new passion and continued leading members in worship for the next two and a half years.

In April 2003, Marshall married his wife, Lori, in the nearby town of Sedona. Then in early 2004, he embarked on another adventure, as baritone for the Gaither Vocal Band, and has been on the road every weekend since.

www.marshallhall.com

**OCTOBER 20, 1908 - MARCH 8, 1989**

# STUART **HAMBLEN**

*Stuart composed such standards as "Until Then," "Teach Me Lord to Wait," and "This Ole House."*

During the 1949 Billy Graham Los Angeles Tent Revival, Stuart Hamblen invited Graham to plug the meeting on his popular radio show. This made *Los Angeles Examiner* headlines. The meeting, held over, resulted in thousands, Stuart included, coming to know Christ. This was the beginning of a long and endearing friendship between the Grahams and Hamblens.

Stuart's talent as singer, composer, and radio-movie personality began in Texas in the 20s. After success in New York with four recordings, Stuart set out for Hollywood, where he made several movies. He was a member of the original *Beverly Hillbillies* cast.

During that time, he wrote and recorded such standards as "Texas Plains," "My Mary," "Golden River," and "Ridin' Old Paint." After he became a Christian, he wrote "It Is No Secret," the first song to cross the barrier from sacred to popular charts. "This Ole House," "Until Then," "Teach Me Lord to Wait," and "Open Up Your Heart," were some of the 225 songs he composed.

Bill and Gloria Gaither often quote the words to his songs and have said that they consider Stuart Hamblen to be one of the great lyricists. Stuart was inducted into the Nashville Songwriter's Hall of Fame and the GMA Hall of Fame. He received the Pioneer Award and has a star on the Hollywood Walk of Fame. He was married for fifty-five years to the lovely lady he referred to as "My Suzy" and had two daughters, Veeva and Lisa, seven grandchildren, and fifteen great-grandchildren.

"When you see me fall asleep, say amen but don't you weep. I've got so many million years that I can't count them." Stuart Hamblen

— Judy Spencer Nelon

www.hamblenmusic.com

# Until Then

Stuart Hamblen

1. My heart can sing when I pause to re - mem - ber,___ A heart-ache here is but a step - ping stone ___ A - long a trail that's wind - ing al - ways up - ward, ___ This trou - bled world is not my fi - nal home, ___ )
2. The things of earth will dim and lose their val - ue ___ If we re - call they're bor - rowed for a while ___ And things of earth that cause the heart to trem - ble, ___ Re - mem-bered there will on - ly bring a smile, ___ ) But UN - TIL
3. This wea - ry world with all its toil and strug - gle ___ May take its toll of mis - er - y and strife ___ The soul of man is like a wait - ing fal - con, ___ When it's re - leased it's des - tined for the skies, ___ )

CHORUS

THEN my heart will go on sing - ing, ___ UN - TIL

# This Ole House

### By Stuart Hamblen

This Ole House once knew my children, This Ole House once knew my wife, This Ole House was home and comfort As we fought the storms of life, This Ole House once rang with laughter This Ole House heard many shouts Now she trembles in the darkness When the lightnin' walks about. *Chorus*

This Ole House is a gettin' shaky, This Ole House is a gettin' old, This Ole House lets in the rain, This Ole House lets in the cold, On my knees I'm gettin' chilly But I feel no fear nor pain, 'Cause I see an angel peekin' Through a broken window pane. *Chorus*

This Ole House is afraid of thunder, This Ole House is afraid of storms, This Ole House just groans and trembles When the night wind flings its arms, This Ole House is gettin' feeble This Ole House is needin' paint, Just like me its tuckered out but I'm a gettin' ready to meet the saints. *Chorus*

My ole hound dog lies a sleepin', He don't know I'm gonna leave, Else he'd wake up by the fireplace And he'd sit there and howl and grieve, But my huntin' days are over Ain't gonna hunt the coon no more, Gabriel done brought in my chariot When the wind blew down the door. *Chorus*

*Chorus:* Ain't a-gonna need this house no longer, Ain't a-gonna need this house no more, Ain't got time to fix the shingles, Ain't got time to fix the floor Ain't got time to oil the hinges Nor to mend the window panes Ain't a-gonna need this house no longer I'm a-gettin' ready to meet the saints.

## MAY 9, 1907 -

# SUZY HAMBLEN

*Suzy was married to Stuart Hamblen for fifty-five years and at ninety-six years of age is still charming on Gaither Homecoming videos.*

The Stuart and Suzy Hamblen story would make a great Christian western novel. At ninety-seven, Suzy, born Veeva Ellen Daniels, in Oklahoma, is just as beautiful and charming as she was when Stuart introduced her on his radio show as "Little Miss Suzy Ashenfella." In 1933, Stuart asked his bride to spend their honeymoon rounding up wild horses in Arizona. She was up to it, all five feet next to this six foot, two inch Texan. She would spend an exciting fifty-five years at his side, which proved to be a match made in heaven. They hosted radio shows, wrote hit songs, entertained, and raised prize horses, just a typical day in the lives of these two colorful characters.

Stuart didn't care much for the business side. He loaded the horses and coon dogs to go into the wild. His little Suzy usually went with him, but sometimes she stayed home to take care of the family and business. It paid off. While on horseback, Stuart happened upon the spot that inspired him to write one of his biggest George Younce (Cathedral) hits: "This Ole House."

Suzy, by creating a cozy home life, should be given credit for another of Stuart's compositions. At midnight, as he heard their grandfather clock striking twelve, the words came, "The chimes of time ring out the news another day is through," the opening line to "It Is No Secret." For twenty-five years, they lived in the Hollywood Hills home they bought from legendary Errol Flynn, and were famous for their parties. They have two daughters, Veeva Suzanne and Lisa Obee, seven grandchildren, and fifteen great-grandchildren. Today Suzy is known by the beloved title of Nana. She still raises prize winning Peruvian Paso horses in Santa Clarita, California.

— Judy Spencer Nelon

## JULY 11, 1947 -

# Larnelle Harris

*Larnelle's gift of music gives voice to what God can do in one man's life.*

Larnelle Harris was born in Danville, Kentucky. He graduated from Western Kentucky University and in 1999 received an honorary doctor of music degree from Campbellsville University.

Over the years, Larnelle has consistently maintained a sound and identity distinctly his own, all the while remaining a vital and hugely popular part of the world of popular music. He has recorded over eighteen albums and received five Grammy and eleven Dove Awards.

Larnelle says, "Every time I read a scripture that I've heard countless times before, I always get something new out of it. Where I am with the Lord and where I am musically have a strong correlation. If I'm standing still in my walk with him, I'm probably standing still creatively. So I'm going to continue the same trek I've tried to stay on all along, panting after the scripture and the things of the Lord, constantly challenging myself to grow in Him – not music. With that as the focus and priority, growth and newness will inevitably be reflected in my music. That's always been the case, because he is the ultimate Creator."

Larnelle doesn't consider the story of his own life to be all that interesting, but the story of what the Lord has done in his life, and in his heart, is the story he has to tell.

Larnelle is a deacon in the church in Louisville, Kentucky, that he and his family have attended for over thirty years. Married to Cynthia and father of Lonnie and Teresa, Larnelle is an avid golfer and an expert ham radio operator. He has composed over thirty songs.

www.larnelle.com

**AUGUST 1, 1939 -**

# JOEL HEMPHILL

*Joel remembers the music of the church always being an important part of his life.*

Joel Wesley Hemphill was born in Fresno, California. He remembers the music of the church being an important part of his life. Joel's father, W. T. Hemphill, loved to sing. He sang when he was happy, and he sang when he was sad. At the age of five, Joel's family moved to West Monroe, Louisiana, where his father founded and pastored a local church. When Joel was in his teens, he played the electric guitar and later served under his father as an associate pastor.

Immediately after high school graduation, one month before his eighteenth birthday, Joel married LaBreeska Rogers after a brief courtship. They soon launched out into an evangelistic ministry. Just before their third child was born, Joel began pastoring a small church in Bastrop. After ten years of fairly normal family and church life, Joel became restless and sought further direction from the Lord. It was at this time that Joel began to write gospel songs. Over the years many groups have recorded the songs that God has inspired Joel to write. Among them are the Blackwood Brothers, the Speer Family, the Gaithers, the Florida Boys, and the Cathedrals.

For twenty-one years, Joel and LaBreeska traveled with their three children, Joey, Trent, and Candy. Now they are back to their beginnings, just the two of them, carrying on the ministry they love and to which they were called, singing and preaching the gospel.

www.thehemphills.com

## FEBRUARY 4, 1940 -

# LaBreeska **Hemphill**

*LaBreeska sang on stage for the first time at the age of nine. Her debut in gospel music was at the famous Ryman Auditorium.*

LaBreeska Rogers was nine years old when she made her debut in gospel music. It was in 1949 on the stage of the famous Ryman Auditorium. She was born in the small mining town of Flat Creek, Alabama. As a member of the Happy Goodman Family, her mother, Gussie Mae, was a sister of Howard, Rusty, and Sam, LaBreeska learned early about the music of the church. Her father Walter Erskine Rogers played the guitar in their church and occasionally accompanied the Goodman Family when they sang specials.

Raised by two grandmothers who loved the Lord and family, LaBreeska grew up in an atmosphere of Christian faith, values, and music.

In 1957, LaBreeska met and married Joel Hemphill. When their first child, Joey, was only six weeks old they began a ministry of singing and preaching. They signed their first recording contract in 1966. The Hemphills are the parents of Joey, Trent, and Candy, who until 1990 traveled and sang with their parents, making them one of the foremost mixed groups in gospel music. LaBreeska and Joel have continued their ministry, just as in the beginning, the two of them. Many of the songs they sing were written by Joel. The group has received six Dove Awards for their efforts, and Joel has been nominated ten times by the GMA as Songwriter of the Year. Familiar titles include "Every Need Supplied," "Master of the Wind," "Consider the Lilies," and "I Claim the Blood."

LaBreeska and Joel have recorded over twenty-seven albums and have had numerous number one and top ten hits.

www.thehemphills.com

**DECEMBER 24, 1927 - JANUARY 4, 2004**

# JAKE HESS

*Always positive...his standard answer was: "Nothin' but fine."*

J ake's vocal style and influence came from his father, who told him singing was talking on key, and the most important thing in a gospel song was the words...and singing them clearly. Jake, born in Mt. Pisgah, Alabama, was the youngest of twelve children.

He started singing at five with the Hess Brothers Quartet, and at sixteen, left home to join the John Daniel Quartet. He met his lifelong friend J. D. Sumner while singing with the Sunny South Quartet. In 1948, as lead singer, he joined with pianist Hovie Lister to organize the Statesmen Quartet. Jake often said, "If there weren't a Hovie Lister, nobody would ever have heard of Jake Hess." In 1963, Jake founded the Imperials, one of the first-ever contemporary groups that began a new era still celebrated today.

Jake was Elvis Presley's all-time favorite singer. Jake and the Imperials sang on Elvis' Grammy-winning gospel album, *How Great Thou Art*. Elvis even tried to sing like Jake, who would later sing at Elvis' own funeral.

In 1952, Jake creatively popped the question to Joyce McWaters, the love of his life, "Would you like to be buried with my people?" She waited until their second date to say, "Yes." Their three children, Becky, Chris, and Jake, Jr. gave them ten grandchildren and one great-grandchild.

At Jake's memorial service, Bill Gaither was emotional when he spoke of his "best friend" and shared how he admired the way Jake gave credit to someone other than himself whenever he was given a compliment. Bill finished his tribute by saying goodbye to one of gospel music's finest gentlemen, "The good news is this...he is singing better than he's ever sung before...and I think he's smiling even more broadly, too."

— Judy Spencer Nelon

www.jakehess.com

**MAY 3, 1971 -**

# JUDY MARTIN HESS

*"My family is the most precious gift God has given me," Judy states.*

Judy Lynn Martin was born in Hayward, California, and at the age of six moved to Hamburg, Arkansas, where she grew up the younger sibling of Jonathan and Joyce. Judy was first influenced by local and regional musical groups, and later by some of the well-known names in southern gospel music.

Those artists made an impression on Judy that impacted her talents already being well-developed at home with her parents' involvement and encouragement. Practicing at home, without a piano of their own, the Martins perfected their signature blend, a blend that would one day place them on the Gaither Homecoming stage, in the White House, on the platform of Carnegie Hall, and on television around the world.

Judy's soothing voice, tight blends, joyful countenance, and genuine smile were integral to the Martins' successes which include eight Dove Awards, a Grammy nomination, and numerous top-selling records, in addition to many hits. Judy, along with the Martins, has set precedents in the southern gospel community, taking traditional harmony and life-altering messages to new audiences, large venues, and many young listeners.

"Choosing a favorite song is like trying to choose a favorite scripture," Judy says. "There are so many songs that have convicted me, blessed me, comforted me, and given me hope...songs are such a major part of my life...when words are not enough, a song can often reach those unreachable places in our hearts and even in our minds.

Judy is married to W. Jake Hess, Jr., son of the legendary and honored singer, Jake Hess. They have three children—Jake Hess, III ("Trip"), Hannah Joyce Hess, and Emily Estelle Hess.

— Celeste Winstead

www.the–martins.com

JULY 13, 1928 -

# LOU WILLS HILDRETH

*Lou has served for twenty years on the Gospel Music Association Board and is one of the founding members of the Southern Gospel Music Guild.*

Lou was born in Memphis, Texas. She was a member of the Texas *First Family of Gospel Music*, the Wills Family. Lou has been a television host, songwriter, publisher, journalist, an industry leader, and served twenty years on the GMA board. She is a passionate supporter of the SGMA Hall of Fame at Dollywood. In 1998, Lou was inducted into the Texas Music Hall of Fame, and in 2004, she was the recipient of the first "James Blackwood Award."

Lou received an honorary doctor of sacred music degree from Louisiana Baptist University, and the Crabb Family recognized her dedication to the youth of gospel music by honoring her with the first "Golden Crabb Award." Lou was the first woman to own a gospel music artist booking agency and was Mark Lowry's first agent. The "Lou Hildreth Award" — recognizing excellence within the gospel music industry is presented during the Diamond Awards at the National Quartet Convention.

Always smiling, Lou is the redhead seen on many of the Gaither Homecoming videos. She is a veteran of gospel television having hosted *Wills Family Inspirational Time* in the 60s, one of the original syndicated shows. In the 70s and 80s, she hosted a daily television show in Nashville and was a Dove Award nominee. Currently, Lou is host of *Hill County Gospel TV* and co-host of *Inside Gospel* with J. P. Miller. Her travels with husband, Howard, are chronicled in the *U. S. Gospel News*. She is the first to give credit to another, and to give praise to God. Lou Wills Hildreth is a shining example of a lifetime committed to sharing the gospel through the power of a gospel song.

— Judy Spencer Nelon

www.gospel-video.com

134

**NOVEMBER 2, 1930 -**
. . . . . . . . . . . . . . . . . . . . . . . . . . . . . . . . . . . . . . . . . . . . . . . . . . . . . . . . . .

# JIM HILL

*Jim composed the song "What a Day That Will Be" and sang with the Golden Keys Quartet and the Statesmen Quartet.*

James Vaughn Hill was born and reared in Portsmouth, Ohio. It was a Christian home where his family enjoyed singing out of a James D. Vaughn convention book around an old upright piano. Jim's name was selected from this book. His father led singing and taught the Bible class at the local Baptist church. When Jim was sixteen, he and three friends were converted at a Baptist camp meeting. They formed the Camp Meeting Boys Trio. It was Jim's first experience of singing before a congregation.

After he was discharged from the Army in 1954, he formed the Golden Keys Quartet. Danny Gaither soon joined the group and added to their success. After they sang for the morning worship service at the National Quartet Convention, all the *pros* were asking where they were getting their new music. Jim told them that Danny's brother, Bill Gaither, was writing it. He laughs now as he remembers their question, "Who is Bill Gaither?"

In 1962, Jim joined the Stamps Quartet, his first professional venture. The Blackwood Brothers had just bought the Stamps Quartet Music Company, in Dallas, and needed a quartet to represent them. As manager, Jim worked with and helped start young singers, such as Terry Blackwood, Mylon LeFevre, Roger McDuff and John Hall. In 1968, he was asked to join the Statesmen Quartet.

Jim feels that the most rewarding of all his accomplishments has been his songwriting. "What a Day That Will Be," and "Precious Jesus," co-written with Gloria Gaither, appear in church hymnals.

He and his wife, Ruth, live in Middletown, Ohio near daughter, Susan, and grandchildren, Melissa and James Michael.

Jim's favorite song is "Great Is Thy Faithfulness."

**OCTOBER 2, 1956 -**
............................................................

# STEPHEN HILL

*Stephen has become a favorite on Gaither Homecoming videos. He is committed to sharing his gifts for the Lord.*

**B**orn in Kirksville, Missouri, Stephen grew up in Greenville, South Carolina. Christian, family man, singer, songwriter, and guitarist, all describe Stephen. He is most known for his appearances on Gaither Homecoming videos and is now concentrating on his solo ministry. As a backup singer, his credits range from Dolly Parton, Aaron Tippin, Hank Williams, Jr., Don McLean, Mark Lowry, Jake Hess, and Ben Speer to Marie Osmond and John Starnes. His versatility and background have served him well in presenting a varied musical palette for his listeners.

Stephen, new to the public, has three solo projects. *Nothing in the World* contains songs written by Stephen and features his latest single, "I Wonder."

Stephen was saved and baptized at the age of seven but fell away from the Lord and church in his teen years. It wasn't until he was grown that Stephen realized he was missing many blessings by a very close margin. One night, he found himself on his knees crying out to the Lord. That cry was heard and Stephen knew the Lord had been waiting for his return. As Stephen looks back on the time he calls his "wasted years," he can see where the Lord had his hand on him and was patient as he guided and corrected him. Stephen is glad that the Lord is long-suffering with us. Stephen says that he is just another example of a "prodigal son come home." He still has a long way to go, but at least he now relies on the Lord for guidance and direction. Stephen remains committed to sharing his gifts for the Lord. "If I get people to focus on Jesus through my talents, I feel I have done my job correctly."

Stephen and his wife, Kathy, have three children, Melody, Miriam, and Caleb.

www.stephenhillmusic.com

**OCTOBER 17, 1953 - JULY 27, 1995**

# KENNY HINSON

*Kenny started singing professionally at fourteen. His compositions included "Call Me Gone" and "I'll Never Be over the Hill."*

Kenneth Duane Hinson was born in Santa Cruz, California. He was the seventh child of Cecil and Stella Hinson. Little Kenny suffered from anemia and severe bronchitis that left his lungs permanently damaged with scar tissue. It was not until he was nearly a teenager that his health improved. Reared in a Christian home, Kenny learned that it would take both persistence and courage to receive what he needed from God.

His father, a minister, shared the knowledge of scripture and faith in Christ, but it was his mother who cultivated Kenny's God-given talent for music. She simply showed him how to place his fingers on the strings of the guitar and that was all that was necessary. It was not long before he joined the ensemble at church.

With brothers, Ronny and Larry, and sister, Yvonne, Kenny helped start the Singing Hinson Family when he was fourteen. Kenny was the guitar player. In the late 1970s, Kenny finally realized that his vocal attributes were more important than his guitar playing abilities. His style of music would come to be known as country gospel music.

Kenny was presented with the award for Favorite Male Vocalist of the Year by *Singing News* in 1976. He was also awarded favorite tenor for three years. He composed three number one songs: "Call Me Gone," "I'll Never Be over the Hill," and "Oasis," as co-writer.

Kenny was married to Debbie. Their children are Kenneth and Amanda.

Since Kenny passed away in 1995, his legendary sound is still with us through the technology of his recordings.

www.officialkennyhinson.homestead.com

**OCTOBER 29, 1946 -**

# RONNY **HINSON**

*Ronny is best known as the composer of the song "The Lighthouse," for which he received the Dove Award for Song of the Year.*

onny was born in Freedom, California, the fifth child of eight. He was reared in a pentecostal preacher's home, with parents who held a tight yet gentle hand on the kids they always referred to as "gifts from God." Ronny attributes his songwriting, both desire and style, to his deeply spiritual upbringing and to the principles and standards demonstrated by his godly parents and expected of him and his siblings.

His experiences, both highs and lows, through life have served to fuel the torch of desire to write his prolific lyrics of the way God will bring a person from the valley to the mountaintop.

Ronny founded the Original Hinsons on December 12, 1967, when he coaxed his three younger siblings to the platform in a small church in Watsonville, California. This began a journey to the top of the gospel music field, where they have impacted countless lives. They are recognized today as "trendsetters," after whom many singers and writers have fashioned their styles.

Ronny has a daughter, Kimberly, a son Bo, and four grandchildren. Kim has a beautiful voice and on occasion has filled in for Bo's wife, Rhonda, in the New Hinsons.

Because of daughter-in-law Rhonda's ability to sing, and because she and Bo are rearing their children in a Christian atmosphere, there are strong indications that there could be a third generation of Ronny's dream that the Hinson version of the gospel in song would echo for years to come.

Some of Ronny's best songs have been recorded and have become number one songs for the New Hinsons. Just a few of these are "Oasis," "Old Ship of Zion," "Speak the Word, Lord."

Today, Ronny has a successful solo ministry.

141

# CLAUDE HOPPER

*Claude says that at low points in his life, God always sends someone to confirm that he is where God wants him to be.*

Claude Hopper was born in Madison, North Carolina, and has become an entrepreneur and legend in the world of southern gospel music. An influential businessman, Claude founded what was originally known as the Hopper Brothers and Connie. Connie later became his wife, and together they are the foundation of one of the most successful and respected family groups in the industry.

In addition to his work with the Hoppers, Claude serves on the board of directors for the National Quartet Convention. He has been an integral part of the Canadian Fan Festival as well as the Great Western Fan Festival. Claude has a rich history of music publishing and founded Hopper Brothers and Connie Publishing. In 1990, he received special recognition from Senator Jesse Helms and Governor Jim Martin for three decades of contributions to the gospel music community. In 1999, Claude received a honorary doctor of music degree. He is a founding member of the North Carolina Gospel Music Hall of Fame.

Claude's leadership has contributed greatly to the Hoppers' ministry and success. He has been greatly influenced personally by the Statesmen, the Blackwood Brothers, Homeland Harmony, the Speer Family, J.D. Sumner and the Stamps, and the Goodman Family. His favorite songs are "Jerusalem," "Here I Am," and "Shoutin' Time."

With appreciation Claude states, "I was able to travel and sing with my brothers for many years, and God has allowed me to continue to travel and sing with my immediate family."

Claude and his wife Connie have two sons, Dean and Mike, and a granddaughter, Karlye.

— Celeste Winstead

www.thehoppers.com

144

## JULY 16, 1940 -

# CONNIE HOPPER

*Connie's spiritual leadership and talents have been instrumental in the Hoppers' successes and honors.*

Connie Hopper is one of the most respected women in southern gospel music. A rock and foundation today for the multiple award-winning Hoppers, Connie Elizabeth Shelton was born in Rockingham County, North Carolina. Early on, she was influenced by the Speer Family, the Goodman Family, Patty Paige, the Platters, and Rosemary Clooney, among others.

Connie is now inspiring fans of her own, not only through her music ministry but through her character and walk of faith. Her presence is one of fortitude and joy; and whether times are good or bad, she seems to "know in whom she has believed." Her sincerity, warmth, and charm have made her a constant friend. Her tears fall quickly with tenderness when she shares subjects close to her heart.

In May of 2003, Connie, also a noted writer, graduated from Oakland City University with a degree in religion. She has penned more than fifty songs throughout her career. She authored a testimonial book, *The Peace That Passeth Understanding*, detailing the story of her bout with cancer and God's healing. In addition she has written a daily devotional book, *Heart of the Matter*, and has spoken at numerous women's conferences.

Connie, whose favorite song is "Who Am I?" has been awarded the Queen of Gospel Music Award twice, and the Favorite Alto of the Year and Favorite Female Vocalist of the Year Awards many times. She received the prestigious *Singing News* Marvin Norcross Award in 1998.

Connie is married Claude Hopper. They are the parents of Dean and Mike and have a granddaughter, Karlye.

— Celeste Winstead

www.thehoppers.com

146

OCTOBER 24, 1962 -

# DEAN HOPPER

*Dean, the driving force behind the scenes for the Hoppers, has recently opened a full-service recording studio near his home.*

Claude Dean Hopper was born in Reidsville, North Carolina, and grew up in Madison, North Carolina. His love and knowledge of southern gospel music began when as a child, he listened to the music of the Happy Goodmans, the Speer Family, and the Cathedrals. Son of Connie and Claude Hopper of the Hoppers Brothers and Connie, it was no surprise that Dean became a member of the group as the drummer until 1981. That year, he became the lead vocalist and after more than twenty years, he continues to share the stage nightly with one of the most legendary southern gospel family groups, the Hoppers.

Dean has received many Lead Vocalist of the Year nominations and was awarded the Outstanding Young Man of America Award. Recently he, and brother Mike, opened a full-service recording, mastering, and digital editing facility, near their home in North Carolina, called The Farm.

Dean married the award-winning Kim Greene, popular soprano for the Greenes. Not long afterward, she joined the Hoppers to round out the family group. Dean and Kim have a daughter, Karlye.

Dean is a businessman and the driving force behind the scenes of the Hoppers. The group has been awarded Favorite Mixed Group more than fifteen times in addition to numerous Soprano of the Year, Female Vocalist of the Year, and Alto of the Year Awards.

Dean shares, "I am very appreciative for the salvation I have in Christ. The opportunities to be used by the Lord are sometimes very obvious and sometimes quite subtle. I thank God for his forgiveness." Dean's favorite song is "The Old Rugged Cross Made the Difference."

— Celeste Winstead

www.thehoppers.com

148

**MAY 25, 1957 -**

# KIM **HOPPER**

*Kim asked Christ into her life at the age of eight and the desire to sing blossomed from there.*

Kim Greene was born in Boone, North Carolina, and grew up singing with her brothers, Tony and Tim. Kim was surrounded by music and knew from an early age that she wanted to sing for her vocation. Her vocals contributed greatly to the success of the Greenes in their early years. They became known for such hits as "It Sure Sounds like Angels to Me" and "There's a Miracle in Me."

After singing with her family for ten years, Kim met Dean Hopper, of the legendary Hoppers. The two were married, and Kim eventually became the fourth member of the Hoppers. Kim's soprano tones took on an entirely new dimension as she prepared to sing in a higher range than she had always sung, taking the Hoppers to even greater distinction with songs such as "Shoutin' Time," "Yes I Am," "Jerusalem," and many more. She has also recorded a solo project *Imagine*, capturing more of the depth and versatility of her vocal skills.

Kim has been awarded Favorite Female Vocalist nine times, as well as Soprano of the Year, eight times. Her favorite song is "These Are They." Musical influences include her family, the Rambos, and Dolly Parton.

Kim does not take family lightly. She describes, "Growing up in a singing family was and still is a special thing. Even at Christmas and other family gatherings, we still have to sing a little. I think maybe God was preparing me for the rest of my life even as a child, because now I sing with my husband, and I plan to hand the tradition on to my children."

Kim continues, "I believe God has given the gift of being able to paint the picture of what I am singing. I am thankful that we can touch the lives we sing to every day."

Kim and Dean are the proud parents of Karlye Jade.

— Celeste Winstead

www.thehoppers.com

150

**JULY 25, 1972 -**

. . . . . . . . . . . . . . . . . . . . . . . . . . . . . . . . . . . . . . . . . . . . . . . . .

# BENJAMIN ISAACS

*Benjamin is the standup bass player for the Isaacs. This musical family has become one of the most important groups in acoustic music.*

Benjamin Joseph Isaacs, affectionately called *Gentle Ben*, is the oldest child of Lily and Joe Isaacs. He was born in Middletown, Ohio, and reared in nearby Morrow. His father, Joe, formed the Calvary Mountain Boys and traveled to area churches. Between 1972 and 1975, Joe and Lily became the parents of Ben, Sonya, and Rebecca.

Young Ben was first influenced musically by his mom and dad. Later, he became interested in the styles of gospel and bluegrass singers such as Tim Caudill, Ricky Skaggs, Roy Husky, Jr., Bob Moore, and Vince Gill. This standup bass player has become one of the most in-demand musicians and has played with Tony Rice, Ralph Stanley, Aubrey Haynie, and Rhonda Vincent.

The Isaacs have been nominated for Grammy and Dove Awards and a host of others. Their story is one of the most compelling in any music field. They have helped build a bridge between bluegrass and southern gospel music combining stunning, folk-influenced harmonies with world-class instrumentation and award-winning songs.

Ben has composed such songs as "The Least I Can Do," "A Portion of Love," and with sister, Sonya, "From the Depths of My Heart." Ben's favorite song is "Go Rest High on the Mountain." He is the father of a daughter, Cameron.

Ben began appearing with the Isaacs on many of the Gaither Homecoming videos, as that groundbreaking series was launched. The Isaacs also have appeared periodically in the Homecoming Concert Series, joining the tour full-time in 2003.

www.theisaacs.com

# LILY ISAACS

*Lily and the Isaacs had huge success with the soundtrack to "O, Brother, Where Art Thou?"*

Lily Fishman Isaacs was born in Munich, Germany, just after the end of World War II. She was the immigrant daughter of Jewish Holocaust survivors from Poland.

Lily was working at Gerde's Folk City in New York when she met Joe Isaacs. This favorite hotspot was where both Bob Dylan and Peter, Paul, and Mary launched their careers. Joe was playing in a group called the Greenbriar Boys. They were married in 1970. Their oldest child, Ben was born two years later, followed in 1974 by Sonya, and by Rebecca in 1975. From 1972 to 1986, Joe headed up a group called Joe Isaacs and the Sacred Bluegrass. During this period, of time the children began picking up a knack for harmony, singing almost before they could talk.

By 1986, they had become a family band, and were calling themselves, the Isaacs. The mixture of Lily's folk music with Joe's traditional mountain, bluegrass style was a big influence in their unique sound.

In the early days, they traveled in a station wagon, then a van, with a cooler of sandwiches. Lily did the booking until in 1992 they went with an outside agent. In 1993, there was a turning point in what proved to be a landmark year. The Isaacs became so popular on the Grand Ole Opry that they were invited back numerous times.

The Isaacs were invited to become part of the Gaither Homecoming videos, and Bill Gaither has stated, "Their performances are fast becoming one of the most anticipated portions of our events."

www.theisaacs.com

**JULY 22, 1974 -**

# SONYA ISAACS

*Sonya has enjoyed solo success with several country singles. With her brother, Ben, she wrote "From the Depths of My Heart."*

**B**orn in Middletown, Ohio, Sonya was reared in Morrow, Ohio. She was influenced musically by Emmylou Harris, Ricky Skaggs, Céline Dion, Ralph Stanley, and New Grass Revival. Sonya is a member her family's southern gospel group, the Isaacs. The group has earned accolades and respect from all corners of the music world. Early on, along with her brother and sister, she learned to play a number of instruments. When the group's mandolin player left, rather than hiring someone to fill the gap, Sonya started playing. According to her mother, Lily, "she worked really hard and learned to play quickly."

Sonya has enjoyed a great deal of solo success, with several country singles, a tour with Vince Gill, and live and studio work with Dolly Parton, Ralph Stanley, Reba McEntire, Brad Paisley, and others. With brother, Ben, she wrote "From the Depths of My Heart," the group's first number one hit, bringing a huge influx of attention and popularity. It was named Song of the Year by both *Gospel News* and the Gospel Voice Awards. Sonya has also written "Stand Still," with sister, Rebecca, as well as "Friend to the End," and "He Understood My Tears." Her favorite song is "The Love of God." In 1994, Sonya was named Horizon Award winner by *Singing News*.

The Isaacs continue their highly popular performances at bluegrass festivals, concert halls, fairs, and churches, making this one of the busiest times of their career. Sonya says, "We are able to cross the lines of style because my family is all acoustic and even bluegrass, yet we do a lot of gospel music. It's pretty neat to be recognized in so many genres of music all at the same time."

www.theisaacs.com

**FEBRUARY 4, 1957 -**

# SUSAN PECK JACKSON

*Susan travels with her sister, Karen, in Karen Peck & New River. Together they have created an award-winning group.*

Born in Gainesville, Georgia, Susan Peck and her sister Karen grew up listening to southern gospel music. Susan made a commitment to the Lord at the age of seven. Her favorite groups were the Kingsmen Quartet, the Happy Goodman Family, and the Hinsons. She has two sisters, Karen Peck Gooch and Sandra Peck. Karen taught Susan to sing alto; and Karen and their mom, Sue, have both been very influential in Susan's singing career. That influence has been multiplied as Susan has been sharing the gospel through music for years with Karen Peck & New River.

The group is known for hits that include "When Jesus Passes By," "God Still Answers Prayer," "Four Days Late," "I Wanna Know How It Feels," "God Likes to Work" and many more. New River has had numerous nominations and Song of the Year awards. Susan was honored for two years consecutively as the SGMA Female Singer of the Year.

In September, 1995, Susan married David Jackson, who is the son of the legendary Shot Jackson, a member of WSM's Grand Ole Opry, and Country Music Hall of Fame inductee. David, owner and builder of the famous "Sho-Bud" guitars, is supportive of Susan's ministry through music. Susan and David have one son, Joseph.

Susan has appeared on several Homecoming videos and is grateful to the Lord for the life she enjoys. She states, "I spent most of my adult years building a career in business and owned a dump truck hauling business. However, in January, 1991, the Lord opened the door for my sister Karen and me to start a new ministry, Karen Peck & New River. Since that time, I've sold my business, gotten married, and now have a son. I thank God for allowing me to sing and travel with my family."

— Celeste Winstead

# BOB JOHNSON

*Bob and his wife Jeanne sang with the Speer Family for eight years. Bob worked for the PTL Television Network for many years.*

Bobby Gray Johnson was born in Greensboro, North Carolina. At fourteen, he accepted Christ. He began singing in high school and later sang with a gospel quartet in his hometown. Bob was influenced musically by Penny and Floyd Andrews and the Gethsemane Quartet, as well as the Speer Family.

Bob joined the Marine Corps in January of 1951 and spent eleven months in Korea. He received the Korean Service Medal with three stars, the Good Conduct Medal, the Presidential Unit Citation, the United Nations Service Medal, and a Purple Heart. He was discharged in January of 1954.

Bob met Jeanne in August of 1959 at a concert in Greensboro. When he saw her, he said, "Anyone that pretty who sings that well should be married to me." They were married about four months later on December 20, 1959.

They joined the Speer Family in September of 1967, and Bob drove the bus and sang with the group. He left the group in 1972 to manage jewelry stores.

In 1978, he went to work for the PTL Television Network, and about eleven years later, Bob and Jeanne started their full-time ministry. In 1991, they formed the Johnson Family Ministries, Inc. where they are still serving, mostly in churches. Bob was ordained into the ministry that same year.

Bob and Jeanne have a daughter, Sonja Rene', who is married to Heath Nestor. They have two daughters, Kylie and Kaylie.

Bob's favorite song is "The Old Rugged Cross."

www.bobandjeannejohnson.org

**JUNE 16, 1941 -**

# JEANNE JOHNSON

*Jeanne is "thankful that when people let us down, the Lord will pick us up and make our lives good."*

Jeanne Poteat was born in Greensboro, North Carolina. Her parents were divorced when she was five years old, and she went to live with her grandparents. One day, she and her brother were dropped off at their grandparents' home, and their parents never came back for them. Jeanne's grandparents took her to church for every service. "That's where I learned that God really loved me." She took piano lessons when her grandmother would save a little of her hard-earned cotton mill earnings. Her teacher, Ethel Reynolds, was a great influence on Jeanne's life. She "picked me up on my lunch break at school, took me home, gave me a lesson, then took me back to school. You think God had a plan for my life?"

Jeanne was also influenced by Floyd and Penny Andrews and the Gethsemane Quartet. She was asked to join the quartet where she met Bob a few months later. Bob and Jeanne were married in 1959. They have a daughter, Sonja Rene´ who is married to Heath Nestor. Sonja and Heath have two daughters, Kylie and Kaylie.

Bob and Jeanne joined the Speer Family in 1967 and were with them for eight years. Many of those years the group received the Dove Award for "Best Mixed Group." They were with the Speers when they introduced Bill and Gloria Gaither's song, "The King Is Coming." Jeanne says it still is one of the high points in their career. Jeanne received the Dove Award for Best Female Singer in 1975.

"One of the best things that has happened to us is the privilege of singing with our Homecoming Friends with Bill and Gloria Gaither. The Lord has blessed us with several recordings.

"My mother and daddy have both passed on, but the good news is they both accepted the Lord. I've never been able to understand their actions, but I have forgiven them."

www.bobandjeannejohnson.org

162

**FEBRUARY 5, 1921 -**

# JIMMY JONES

*Jimmy was the bass singer with the LeFevres and is famous for his recitations on the "Poetry Corner."*

**B**orn on a farm in Allen County, Kentucky, James Edward Jones was the ninth of the eleven children of James and Bertha Jones. Jimmy grew up in a singing family that was taken, not sent, to church every Sunday. At thirteen, as the senior member, he sang lead in the Midget Quartet. Sometimes the group's mode of travel was a two-horse wagon.

Jimmy's professional singing career began in March, 1944, at KTHS radio station in Hot Springs, Arkansas, with Otis Echols and the Melody Boys. In 1951, Jimmy moved to Dallas, Texas, and joined the Rangers Quartet to sing bass. His next move was to Atlanta along with his brother, Brownie, to form the Deep South Quartet. This group worked the regular concert circuit until 1956, when they moved to Washington, D.C., to perform with Jimmy Dean on his popular television show.

In 1957, Jimmy joined the LeFevres. At this time, the Gospel Singing Caravan which toured throughout the United States and Canada was formed. During this period, the Le Fevres produced and hosted the nationally syndicated *Gospel Singing Caravan Show*. It was on this show that Jimmy performed his famous recitations in a segment called the "Poetry Corner."

Jimmy retired from the road in 1968 to live in Atlanta where he owned and operated the LeFevres Sing Publishing Company, later selling it to Rex Nelon. He was presented the Living Legend Award by the Grand Old Gospel Reunion in 1995.

Jimmy says, "The Lord has blessed me with good health and good friends and the privilege in my latter years to be a part of the Bill Gaither Homecoming Friends. I thank God every day for the joy of singing and the wonderful people with whom I have had the pleasure of working and worshiping."

APRIL 30, 1938 -

# LILLIE KNAULS

*Lillie is loved and known for her big, encouraging smile, the lovely hats, pretty face, and great voice that can sing any style.*

In 1970, Lillie was an original member of the Edwin Hawkins Singers, who sold over a million albums of "Oh Happy Day," and was inducted into the GMA Hall of Fame in 2001. Lillie was a beloved part of the Audrey Mieir Sings, and it was this friend and mentor who encouraged her to retire from the telephone company in San Jose, California, and go into full-time music ministry. Lillie lived for ten years in Hawaii, from where she could travel easily to the Orient. Lillie has referred to herself as a *Musicianary*. Her first recording on Manna Records in California introduced her talent to the Gaithers. She was the the first artist on their new label, Paragon Records, with Bob Mackenzie as producer.

A favorite on the Gaither Video Series, she is loved and known for her big, encouraging smile, the lovely hats, and pretty face with the great voice that can sing any style. Lillie says that when she was invited to a Homecoming taping, she thought she would wear a hat. Folks began telling her how much they liked it. Some sixty videos later, she says, "I'm known as the 'hat lady.'" Out of that has come the opportunity for Lillie to do "Hats-on Breakfasts and Luncheons with Miss Lillie." She has even written a song called "Hattitude."

Bill Gaither knows he can count on Lillie when he suddenly hands her the microphone on any song, even without notice. Lillie is a gifted and popular soloist and speaker, around the world!

— Judy Spencer Nelon

www.misslillie.com

**MARCH 2, 1912 - DECEMBER 9, 1988**

# ALPHUS LE FEVRE

*Alphus, with the Le Fevres, was inducted into the GMA Hall of Fame and into the SGMA Hall of Fame in 2002.*

Alphus Le Fevre was born in Smithville, Tennessee, to Silas and Martha Le Fevre, the second of ten children, all of whom had biblical names and liked music. With his older brother Urias playing banjo, sister Maude, guitar, and Alphus, with his new fiddle, the Le Fevre Trio was born. In the early 1930s, Urias and Alphus attended Bible Training School, now Lee University. Urias married Eva Mae Whittington in 1934 and she joined the two brothers, reorganizing the Le Fevre Trio. They took time off during the war when Alphus was in the army, and Urias was in the navy. The two brothers accidentally ran into each other in the Philippines and were able to spend about a week together.

After the war, the trio continued where they left off. In June 1950, Alphus married his sweetheart, Ellender Smith, of Atlanta. They have two children, Maria Lee and Scott Alphus, and four grandchildren.

Later, the Le Fevres, as a quartet, with Urias and Eva Mae's son, Pierce, introducing his Uncle Alphus, caught on with the fans and stuck. Uncle Alf's accomplishments were immense. As a musician, he played guitar, fiddle, banjo, piano, dobro, steel guitar, and mandolin, and was famous for his accordion music at concerts. As an arranger, he wrote four- to eight-part vocal harmony for over five hundred songs. He wrote songs and arranged standards such as "Keep on the Firing Line," and "Must I Go Empty Handed?" He also encouraged his nephew, Mylon, with his song, "Without Him."

No one had a bigger smile or was a kinder person than Alphus. Eva Mae remembers her brother-in-law as a person who encouraged others and never spoke an unkind word about anyone. He would say, "If you can't say something nice, then don't say anything." His life and talent contributed to the Le Fevres' Golden Era!

— Judy Spencer Nelon

168

## AUGUST 17, 1917 -

# EVA MAE LE FEVRE

*Eva Mae was named "Queen of Gospel Music" and was the first living woman inducted into the GMA Hall of Fame.*

Eva Mae Whittington was born in McCall, South Carolina. Her father was a minister and at the age of five, Eva Mae began singing at her father's street-corner services. By six, she would sit on her father's lap to play the church's organ while he pumped the pedals.

Eva Mae was eight when she met Urias and Alphus LeFevre. They had arrived at her father's church to put on a concert. Although Urias was sixteen and Eva Mae was only eight, he knew he had met his future wife. Eight years later, in 1939, Eva Mae and Urias were married and with Alphus formed the LeFevre Trio.

During World War II, while Urias and Alphus were serving their country, Eva Mae sang with the Homeland Harmony Quartet. After the war, the trio was reunited and traveled throughout North America with their wonderful southern gospel sound. During this time, Mylon was born, joining siblings, Pierce, Meurice, and Andrea. Later another daughter, Monteia, was born.

Notables, Jim Waites and Hovie Lister, performed with the group for awhile. By 1954, with popularity growing for the LeFevres, Eva Mae was named Queen of Gospel Music. By the late 1950s the LeFevres were living in Atlanta when Jimmy Jones and Rex Nelon joined the group. The weekly television program, the *Gospel Singing Caravan Show* ushered in the golden era for the LeFevres.

By 1977, Eva Mae retired from traveling, saying she was going to stay home and enjoy retirement with Urias. At this time the LeFevres became the Rex Nelon Singers. The next year, Eva Mae was given the unique honor of being the first living woman ever inducted into the GMA Hall of Fame. In 1988, she was inducted into the Georgia Music Hall of Fame. She has also been inducted into the SGMA Hall of Fame. Bill Gaither has stated that Eva Mae's actions at the first Homecoming taping sparked the beginning of the video series.

www.evamae.com

**OCTOBER 6, 1944 -**

# MYLON LEFEVRE

*Mylon has become a preacher and teacher. Worshiping God has become his lifestyle.*

**M**ylon LeFevre was born into a gospel singing family in Gulfport, Mississippi. In June, 1962, at the age of seventeen, Mylon joined the army. His pay as a private was eighty-four dollars a month. His mom, Eva Mae, and dad, Urias, were scheduled to sing at Ellis Auditorium in Memphis, Tennessee, for the Gospel Quartet Convention. Mylon's mother asked Mylon to come and sing his recently composed song, "Without Him." Mylon hitchhiked the five hundred miles from Fort Jackson, South Carolina, in his army uniform. Unknown to the LeFevres, Elvis Presley was planning to record a gospel album and came to the concert to choose some songs. Elvis loved "Without Him" and recorded it on his first gospel album, *How Great Thou Art.* Over the next few years, the song was recorded by over one hundred artists.

At the age of twenty-five, Mylon was fired by his family because of his long sideburns. He formed the group that became the Atlantic Rhythm Section. He eventually got involved with drugs. In 1980, Mylon attended a concert by the 2nd Chapter of Acts where he rededicated his life. He quit rock and roll, became a janitor at his church, and started going to Bible studies. In 1981, he formed Mylon and Broken Heart, a Christian rock band that has led 211,000 people to a decision for Christ.

Since 1980, Mylon has released twelve CDs, traveled over two million miles, been honored with a Grammy Award and two Dove Awards, and sold more than a million records. In 1993, he was called to preach the gospel.

Mylon is now a preacher and teacher and worshiping God has become his lifestyle. It is Mylon's desire that all would "taste and see that the Lord is good and his mercy endures forever."

www.mylon.org

# JANUARY 25, 1910 - AUGUST 21, 1979

# URIAS LE FEVRE

*Urias was the driving force behind the "golden era" of the Le Fevres.*

**U**rias Le Fevre was a professional gospel singer who managed the Le Fevres from 1921 to 1964. Urias came from a naturally talented family. He and his brother, Alphus, attended what now is Lee College in Cleveland, Tennessee. As a part of the Bible Training School Quartet Number Two, they began their long journey as one of the most successful and innovative gospel music groups.

Eva Mae Whittington, an accomplished alto singer and piano player, joined the duo after she married Urias in 1934. Atlanta became home for the Le Fevres in 1939. The Le Fevre Trio began performing on Radio WGST and soon expanded to include family members and other professional singers and musicians. They were called the Le Fevres.

Urias was known for creating some of the *firsts* in gospel music. He was responsible for having the first public address system as part of the concert. 78 RPM recordings were made of the Le Fevres in the 1940s which helped spread the popularity of the group. By 1950, television provided even more exposure for the group. It was then that the Le Fevres began performing on WAGA-TV in Atlanta. They later created the *Gospel Singing Caravan Show*, the first gospel music television show in syndication and on concert tour.

Urias can be credited with launching many young gospel music singers. At their career's high point, the Le Fevres were traveling 100,000 miles, and holding 250 concerts a year.

The Le Fevres retired in the late 1970s and sold their music businesses to Rex Nelon, a longtime member of the group. Urias and Eva Mae were inducted into the GMA Hall of Fame, as well as the SGMA Hall of Fame in 1997.

## SEPTEMBER 17, 1926 - DECEMBER 28, 2001

# HOVIE LISTER

*His flair for showmanship put Hovie Lister and the Statesmen on top.*

Hovie Lister was born in Greenville, South Carolina. He began playing the piano at age six. By fourteen, he was accompanying the Lister Brothers Quartet, a group made up of his father and uncles. Later, he played for the LeFevre Trio, Homeland Harmony, and the Rangers Quartet. By 1948, he organized the Statesmen Quartet. They took the country by storm with Hovie the driving force, with his flair for showmanship, style of piano playing and his enthusiasm as master of ceremonies, which usually sounded more like preaching and certainly stirred one's soul.

Hovie determined to have the best of the best in this new quartet that finally included Jake Hess, "Big Chief" Wetherington, Rosie Rozelle, and Doy Ott. Among their biggest hits were "Get Away Jordan" and "O What a Savior." They recorded dozens of albums.

In 1980, Hovie was involved in the formation of the Masters V. This group included Hovie, Jake Hess, James Blackwood, J. D. Sumner, and Rosie Rozelle. Needless to say, they were an instant hit! Health problems forced this group off the road. With the help of Bill Gaither, the Statesmen made a comeback in 1992.

In 1993, Hovie was diagnosed with throat cancer. He had surgery on his birthday and by the spring of 1994 was back out on the road, healthy again.

On the Memphis Homecoming video, Hovie made everyone laugh when he said, "Had I known that young Bill Gaither was going to grow up into the highly successful man we all know now, I would have been much nicer to him back then." However, I would say: "Being nice, came easy for Hovie Lister."

Hovie was married to Ethel, the love of his life, and was the father of Lisa and Hovie, Jr. (Chip), and grandfather of two.

— Judy Spencer Nelon

SEPTEMBER 8, 1921 -

# MOSIE LISTER

*Mosie was an original member of the Statesmen Quartet. He has written hundreds of songs that have blessed many lives.*

Few songwriters have enjoyed the success attained by Mosie Lister. Though in his eighties, he continues to write better than ever. Engage him in conversation and he'll be sure to tell you that he's "not retired!" "'Til the Storm Passes By," "Then I Met the Master," "How Long Has It Been," "I'm Feelin' Fine," and "His Hand in Mine" are but a few of the hundreds of songs that have emerged from his prolific pen.

Born and raised in Cochran, Georgia, Mosie studied English and music in college. Mosie credits Mr. Adger M. Pace, an early teacher, with words of wisdom about writing music. He quoted, "Be sure the tune can be whistled. Use a title people can remember. Start well and end well with something meaningful in the middle."

By the late 1940s, Mosie had worked with a number of groups, including a brief tenure as an original member of the Statesmen Quartet. However, as his songs began to find favor, Mosie retired from the road to devote all of his time to songwriting.

In 1953, he founded his own Mosie Lister Publishing Company, later merging with Lillenas Publishing. During his career, Mosie was known for his ability to draw from a variety of musical styles, always with strong Bible-inspired, Christian lyrics. As a result, gospel and secular artists such as George Beverly Shea, Jimmy Davis, Elvis Presley, and Porter Waggoner have recorded his songs. His two favorite songs are "Amazing Grace" and "Holy, Holy, Holy," mostly because of the impact of their message. Today, Mosie and his wife, Martha, make their home in Brandon, Florida.

— Bob Crichton

JUNE 24, 1958 -

# MARK LOWRY

*Mark is known for his comedy. Since he and Buddy Greene wrote "Mary, Did You Know?" it has become a seasonal standard.*

**M**ark Alan Lowry was born and grew up in Houston, Texas. Since age eleven he has been singing, recording albums, and making videos. In the years just after graduation, he traveled to every Independent Baptist church throughout the country. At one time, his agent had booked Mark in forty-three cities in forty-one days! His comedy routine developed when he had to fill gaps in concerts while soundtracks were being changed. He made his audiences laugh as he told stories of his life and testimony.

For thirteen years beginning in 1988, Mark sang baritone with the Gaither Vocal Band. Mark's rapport with Bill Gaither during a concert was a hit and became a highlight when the Homecoming tour came into being. Mark has been featured on all of the Homecoming videos, often in a co-staring role with Bill.

In 1984, Mark wrote a series of questions to be used between scenes of a Christmas play. Six years later, Buddy Greene wrote music for Mark's lyrics and a beautiful Christmas song was born. Over thirty different artists have recorded "Mary, Did You Know?" including Michael English, Kenny Rogers, Wynonna Judd, Natalie Cole, Donny Osmond, and of course, Mark himself.

Mark has recorded six comedy and music videos. Four of them have gone gold, while two are platinum. His most recent video, *On Broadway*, remained at the top of the Billboard Charts for weeks.

Mark's most recent project, *Some Things Never Change* includes some of his favorite songs such as "All That Matters to the Lord," "Jesus Laughing," "He's There," and "Isn't It Amazing?"

Mark's father, Charles, is a Lynchburg, Virginia, attorney. His Mother, Beverly, speaks and sings at various conferences. She has been featured on two of Mark's recordings.

www.marklowry.com

180

**DECEMBER 7, 1920 - JUNE 30, 1954**

# BILL LYLES

*Bill sang bass with the Blackwood Brothers Quartet until a plane crash took his life in 1954.*

**B**ill was killed in a plane crash with R W Blackwood in 1954 near Clanton, Alabama. A crowd of 5,000 attended their funeral in Memphis, Tennessee. Bill had three sons, Bill, Jr., Gary and Curtis. Bill, Jr. remembers getting post cards from his dad when he traveled.

Here is what Bill, Jr. says, "My dad was born James William Lyles, in Burning Bush, Georgia. He was the fourth of seven children. I don't really know where or when his interest in gospel music began, but I do know that he sang with the Hamilton Quartet in Chattanooga, Tennessee, and also with the Swanne River Boys.

"He and my mother were married in June, 1940, and I came along in October, 1941. They met in church in Chattanooga where Daddy sang in the choir. We were living in Stone Mountain, Georgia, when Daddy was contacted by James Blackwood with an offer to join the Blackwood Brothers Quartet for a salary of seventy dollars a week. I still have the telegram.

"He never wrote any music nor garnered any awards that I know of. He just happened to be the best and smoothest bass singer ever. Many, many folks have told me so, and I just happen to agree. He was a good Christian man who loved his family very much.

"Whenever he returned from a long trip, my brother and I would get up to see him regardless of the time. He always had a gift for us. I remember seeing the joy in his face during those times. When he died it was such a great loss to my mother, Ruth, and I never understood till after she died and read notes tucked in the Bible. I'll always wonder what life would have been like had he remained alive, but God in his infinite mercy and love took care of us."

— Bill Lyles, Jr.

**MAY 19, 1970 -**

# JONATHAN MARTIN

*Jonathan and his sisters have appeared on many Homecoming videos and with top of the chart recordings have received six Dove Awards.*

**W**ylma and J. W. Martin, reared Joyce, Jonathan, and Judy in rural Hamburg, Arkansas, in an eight hundred square-foot cabin without electricity or indoor plumbing. To pass the time away, the young siblings began singing together and were coached by their musical mom who had no formal training. Jonathan recalls practicing bass guitar against a hollow interior door and using a car battery to listen to the radio, where the youngster picked up harmony by ear. He remembers having to ration listening on Fridays and Saturdays to save the battery.

Little did they know that in just a few years, friends Mark Lowry and Michael English, would seize Gloria Gaither at a video taping to audition the "Martins" in the women's restroom where the acoustics were just right. By noon, the next day, Bill had invited them to sing "He Leadeth Me" on the *Precious Memories* video.

In 1988, their home state of Arkansas honored the trio with the distinguished Governor's Award of Excellence. The group is one of the most recognized in gospel music with their unique sound, which is affectionately referred to as *Martin music*. Favorites include "Grace," "Out of His Great Love," and an a cappella rendition of "The Doxology." It has been more than the family could have ever imagined, even an invitation to sing for President George W. Bush at the White House.

Jonathan's faith and family values have sustained him during life's challenges. His testimony is one of courage, grace, and God's faithfulness. His songs reflect the promises that God has for all of us. His favorite scripture with wife Dara and his four children, Halea, Taylor, Michael, and Olivia is James 1:2, "Count it all joy!"

— Judy Spencer Nelon

www.the-martins.com

184

**JANUARY 6, 1968 -**

# JOYCE **MARTIN**

*Joyce's determination for excellence has been a driving force. Her relaxed, heartfelt sharing, and laughter have inspired countless people.*

Wylma Joyce Martin, named for her mother, was born in Bastrop, Louisiana, and grew up close by in Hamburg, Arkansas. Music became a central part of Joyce's life at an early age as she and her two siblings, Judy and Jonathan, were taught to sing by their mother.

"She would teach us the old hymns," describes Joyce, "around the piano at church and made sure we knew our parts. We couldn't afford a piano, so we had to practice everything a cappella. That is how our blend grew to be tight."

That blend would one day be a signature sound for one of the most innovative groups of its time, the Martins, who epitomize what southern gospel harmony is all about, yet with their unique twist added to it. Featured regularly on the Gaither Homecoming videos and concerts, the Martins quickly became a crowd favorite with not only a moving testimony to older individuals but also as an inspiration to many young artists of the genre's future.

Joyce, influenced musically by Patti LaBelle and Wynonna Judd, has a voice that rings out with unbridled passion and forte. Her talent as an emcee has given new life to the performance aspects of southern gospel music.

Along with Judy and Jonathan, Joyce has received a Grammy nomination and eight Dove Awards, including several Southern Gospel Song of the Year honors.

Joyce especially enjoys time with her family. "I have two beautiful children," Joyce states. "Trey and Mae are little miracles that remind me every day that God is faithful, and He cares about the personal desires of our hearts."

— Celeste Winstead

www.the–martins.com

186

**FEBRUARY 1, 1955 -**

# BABBIE MASON

*Becoming one of the most exciting Christian artists in the nation has not changed Babbie's down to earth approach to life.*

Like so many female vocalists that preceded her, Babbie Yvett Robie Wade began her music education in the church. It is there she allowed the seeds of faith to be planted, nurtured, and there they bore fruit. As a preacher's daughter from Jackson, Michigan, Babbie says, "I don't remember a time that I didn't love the Lord. It was easy to fall in love and commit to Christ. I watched my parents." Babbie's parents, George and Georgie Wade, served in one church for nearly forty years. Shortly after giving her life to Christ at the age of eight, Babbie began serving as church pianist and choir director and did so for sixteen years. There, Babbie began experiencing first-hand, the joys of leading others in worship.

This dedication to the Lord serves as a firm foundation in her home. The Masons enjoy working together and consider themselves perfect examples of how God can use a husband and wife team to compliment each other's strengths and weaknesses. Babbie says, "Our differences have proven to be the strength in our relationship both at home and on the road."

Living in Georgia, Babbie and husband, Charles, make it a priority to be there for their sons, Jerry and Chaz.

Babbie's compositions have been recorded by such artists and groups as Larnelle Harris, CeCe Winans, Helen Baylor, Albertina Walker, Scott Wesley Brown, Truth, and the Brooklyn Tabernacle Choir. Her works have been in countless print projects, including choral octavos, musicals, hymnals, and worship chorus books.

A teacher at heart, Babbie is compelled to share her knowledge with young musicians as adjunct professor of songwriting at local colleges. She and Charles mentor hundreds of upstart musicians at the annual Babbie Mason Music Conference.

www.babbie.com

**JANUARY 26, 1943 -**

# GARY MCSPADDEN

*Gary says that as a pastor and gospel singer, God's Word and God's Music have been and are the theme of his life.*

Gary Michael McSpadden was born in Mangum, Oklahoma, and grew up in Lubbock, Texas. Early musical influences in Gary's life were the Statesmen Quartet, the Blackwood Brothers, the Oak Ridge Quartet, Jake Hess, and Elvis. As a teenager, Gary dreamed of being involved in gospel music. He joined the Statesmen to fill in for Jake Hess and soon after became a member of the Oak Ridge Boys. Later Gary, with Jake Hess, formed the Imperials.

For the first three years that Gary was lead singer for the Bill Gaither Trio, he and his father were joint pastors of a church in Fort Worth, Texas. Over the years, Bill, Gloria, and Gary recorded some of the world's best known and most loved gospel songs.

Gary was honored when the groups he had sung with, the Imperials and the Bill Gaither Trio, were inducted into the GMA Hall of Fame. After Gary left the Trio to pursue a solo career, he recorded thirteen albums and also began writing songs. "Jesus Lord to Me," "Hallelujah Praise the Lamb," and "Jesus Be Jesus in Me" have become familiar choruses sung in our churches.

Gary says, "As a child, I watched and listened to a wonderful man of God preach and live what he believed. That man was my father. What he believed, preached, and lived, was the Bible...the Word of God. I was given a special heritage...the preaching and singing of the Gospel of Jesus Christ. My heritage and call is to go into all the world and preach the gospel to every one. I have tried to do exactly what Christ commanded.

Gary and his wife, Carol, have two children, Shawn and Michelle, and five grandchildren.

www.garymcspadden.com

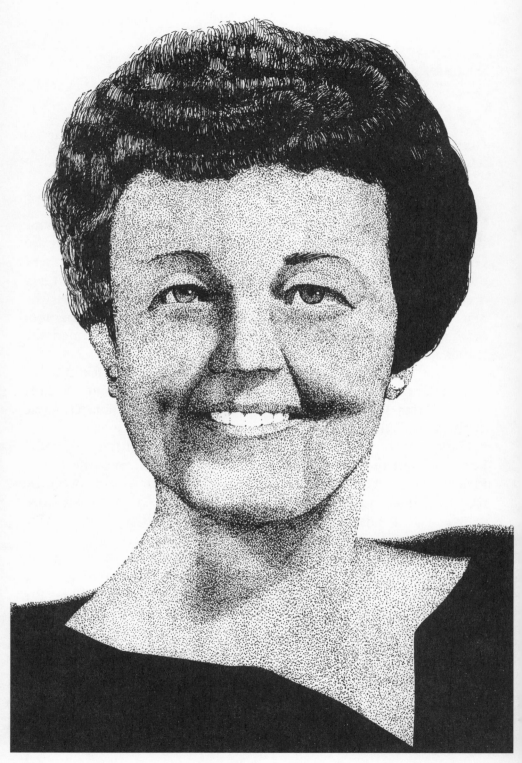

190

**MAY 12, 1916 - NOVEMBER 5, 1996**

# AUDREY MIEIR

*Audrey composed hundreds of songs including "His Name Is Wonderful," known around the world in many languages.*

In 1926, little ten-year-old Audrey Wagner sat on the balcony stairs of Angelus Temple in Los Angeles, California, as Aimee Semple McPherson came to the platform with great chords of music filling the place, swelling from the magnificent organ, the Silver Band, and the choir. Fifty-two hundred people filled the auditorium. Hollywood stars and politicians rubbed elbows with common folks. Audrey dreamed of someday being on that stage and soon she was. She attended LIFE Bible College, and on January 1, 1936, married the love of her life, Charles Mieir, with Aimee Semple McPherson officiating. God, Aimee's style and music inspired Audrey to compose. She was always grateful to Aimee Semple McPherson, her mentor.

After her mother's untimely death, Audrey went through a dry period and wrote no songs for a year. One night, she asked God to forgive her and early in the morning she was comforted with the words that she began to compose and sing: "I'll Never Be Lonely Again." A choir director, composer, and arranger, she trained others and introduced many new, young artists, including her beloved Lillie Knauls and Andrae' Crouch, who affectionately referred to her as his *great white mama*. They credit Audrey with much of their success. She introduced them to her lifelong publisher, Tim Spencer at Manna Music, where both obtained contracts, and Andrae' published his first song, "The Blood Will Never Lose Its Power."

Audrey developed a passion for abandoned Korean-American children and devoted her life to the Mieir Havens in Korea. She was instrumental in bringing thousands of children to America for adoption. Audrey and Charles had a son, Michael, an adopted son, Mark, and an adopted daughter, Liane from Korea.

— Judy Spencer Nelon

**JULY 8, 1955 -**

# JOHNNY MINICK

*Once pianist and arranger for the Happy Goodman Family, Johnny is a busy pastor who still maintains a limited concert schedule.*

Born in Little Rock, Arkansas, Johnny Minick grew up in the home of Christian parents who nurtured him in Godly traditions. At three, he started singing and playing the guitar, and by six had developed an interest in the piano and began classical training. After winning several regional and national piano competitions, he became the pianist and arranger for the Happy Goodman Family. His classical and jazz background immediately influenced the direction of the Goodman recordings.

Striking a balance between full-time music ministry and the calling to preach was difficult. In 1977, Johnny left the Goodmans to pursue the pulpit ministry he had begun at age twelve. After some years as a successful evangelist, he pioneered a church in Little Rock. During those years, Johnny wrote several songs for his family group, the Johnny Minick Family, that charted nationwide.

In 1992, Johnny and his family moved to Smyrna, Tennessee, to pioneer another church, River of Life. After the loss of Rusty and Sam, the Goodmans were looking for new direction. Frequently they would drive to Smyrna to hear their friend, Johnny Minick, preach. They sang in a few of those services. After appearing on Gaither videos, the Goodman Family began singing again and continued until Howard's death in 2002. Johnny's son, Aaron picked up Howard's microphone and kept the group together until Vestal's death in 2003.

Johnny and his wife, Sherry, continue to pastor the River of Life Church in Smyrna. He is still recording and busy with a limited concert schedule along with revivals and special events.

Johnny's favorite songs are "The Love of God" and "The Eastern Gate."

**FEBRUARY 25, 1932 -**

# ARMOND MORALES

*In 1963, Armond began singing with the Weatherford Quartet. Two years later, he was singing bass for the original Imperials Quartet.*

**B**orn in Huntington Park, California, Armond was reared in the Assembly of God Church in Maywood, California. He began singing in the youth choir before joining the adult choir. Armond says "I sang my first solo when I was about fourteen years old. I started out as a tenor until my voice changed and you know the rest."

Armond's father, Alfred Morales came from the Philippines, met and married his mother, Alice Riddle. They had four children, Armond, Alice, Kenneth, and Pam.

Armond has been involved in gospel music since the early 50s and started singing with the Weatherford Quartet in southern California. He was an original member of the Imperials when they were formed in 1964. His brilliant career has included working with Elvis, Jimmy Dean, Carol Channing, and Pat Boone.

The groups Armond has sung with have received Grammy and Dove Awards. He was honored when the Imperials were inducted into the GMA Hall of Fame.

Armond has four children. The three from his first marriage are Bryan, Lisa, and Tracey. He married his wife, Bonnie in November, 1970. They have a son, Jason, who sings with the Imperials. Jason and his wife Erin have a daughter, Madeline, born in July 2004. Armond says, "She is the apple of Poppy's eye."

The song Armond loves most is "Praise the Lord." Countless people have been touched by that song including Armond, himself. He has traveled millions of miles doing what he loves to do most, singing and ministering the gospel of Jesus Christ.

Today, Armond sings with some former members of the Imperials in a group called the Classic Imperials.

— Bonnie Morales

www.theimperials.org

196

**AUGUST 11, 1937 -**

# JOE MOSCHEO

*Joe, an original member of the Imperials, has throughout his career been a leader in the gospel music industry.*

Joe A. Moscheo II grew up in Albany, New York, and moved to Nashville in 1964. Through the 60s and 70s he worked as a studio musician and record producer. As a result of his relationship with Elvis during that time, he has been involved in many recording projects and television events. Joe was associate producer for *He Touched Me — The Gospel Music of Elvis Presley*, which was a joint project between the Elvis Presley Estate and Gaither Television Production. As a member of the Imperials, Joe worked with Elvis on stage and in the recording studio from 1968 to 1972, both as a singer and keyboard player. He has maintained a lasting relationship with the Presley family and is frequently a part of their ongoing celebrations of Elvis around the world.

In 1978, Frances Preston, then president and CEO of BMI, hired Joe to work with songwriters and music publishers. During his sixteen years at BMI, Joe had the pleasure of being involved in all aspects of the music industry, while cultivating a close relationship with many organizations outside the music field. He produced the Dove Awards for eight years and, as a member of the Imperials, was inducted into the GMA Hall of Fame. In 2004, Joe was executive producer of the GMA Hall of Fame Awards which aired on the TBN cable network.

From 1994 to 1996, Joe had his own artist management company where he worked with BeBe and CeCe Winans, Michael English, Wynonna and Naomi Judd, and several other contemporary Christian artists.

Joe retired in January 2003, from Entertainment/Music Banking and now pursues his hobbies of tennis, golf, and painting. He has been married to Judy since February of 1984 and has four children and five grandchildren.

197

**OCTOBER 23, 1968 -**

# BUDDY MULLINS

*Buddy sang lead with the Gaither Vocal Band and has written many number one gospel and contemporary Christian songs.*

**K**enneth Harold Mullins, or as most people know him, "Buddy," was born in Trenton, Tennessee. He began traveling full time with his family as a child of eight. Singing quickly became his life's pursuit. With each year, he seemed to be climbing up a ladder of success and recognition. Then one day, the ladder fell apart and he had to come to terms with the difference in *singing* about his faith and truly *living* it.

God wanted Buddy to pursue him, not just a singing career. Through this time, God made clear to him the most important stage he would ever perform on was not in front of audiences of thousands, but of three people within the walls of his home. God has been gracious and given him a new platform of solo ministry.

Buddy has been influenced by Kenny Hinson, Ronnie Milsap, Russ Taff, Michael English, and Don Henley. The groups he has been a part of are: the Mullins, Mullins & Co., the Gaither Vocal Band, and Sunday Drive. In 1992, the Mullins won the award for Favorite New Group from *Singing News*. Buddy has written number one songs for southern gospel and contemporary Christian music. He was the lead vocalist for the Gaither Vocal Band from 1993 to 1995. His band, Sunday Drive, toured with Josh McDowell Ministries and various other contemporary groups.

Buddy is married to Kerri Anne, and they have two daughters, Victoria Scarlet and Jaclyn Olivia.

Buddy says, "No stage will ever elevate itself above my walk with Christ and my family."

www.buddymullins.com

200

MARCH 8, 1944 -

# JIM MURRAY

*While Jim sang with the Imperials, they received five Grammy Awards and fifteen Dove Awards.*

**B**orn in Lansing, Michigan, Jimmie Kenneth Murray has always loved good, old-fashioned southern gospel music. While growing up, Jim immersed himself in musical opportunities.

After studying voice for two years at Michigan State University, Jim became a member first of the Melodairs Quartet, and later the Ambassadors Quartet. While Jim was singing with the Orrell Quartet in 1966, Jake Hess heard that rich tenor voice and invited him to join the newly-formed Imperials. During the twenty years Jim was with the Imperials, he had the opportunity to sing backup for Elvis, Pat Boone, and Carol Channing.

Over the two decades that Jim was with the Imperials, they produced fifty albums and received five Grammy Awards and fifteen Dove Awards. After the Imperials shifted from traditional four-part harmony that had been their trademark to a more pop-style, Jim decided to leave the group.

By 1988, Bill Gaither invited Jim to join the Gaither Vocal Band. His wonderful tenor voice shone on such favorites as "Wings" and "A Few Good Men," and being featured on the Homecoming series gave him an opportunity to sing four-part harmony again.

Jim says, "I've known Bill and Gloria for many years, and I have always respected their integrity. It was a joy to be part of the Gaither team, especially the now historic video series."

Following surgery, Jim thought he would never sing again. Thanks to his doctors and countless prayers, the Lord has allowed him to continue to minister with his voice. Today, Jim and his wife, Lorretta, live in Hawaii where he has reunited with his friends Terry Blackwood, Armond Morales, and Sherman Andrus to form the Classic Imperials.

www.jimmurrayministry.com

**OCTOBER 7, 1944 -**

# JUDY SPENCER NELON

*Judy is the first woman to be president of the Southern Gospel Music Guild. She also serves on the board of directors for GMA and SGMA.*

Born in Valdosta, Georgia, Judy, Sharon, and Linda, the Peck sisters, began to harmonize at a young age. Their inspiration came from hearing their favorite groups, the Blackwood Brothers, the Statesmen, the Le Fevres, who later became the Rex Nelon Singers, and Doris Akers, in their preacher dad's record store in Columbus, Georgia. Little did Judy know that one day she would not only become friends with, but would also be the publisher, as vice-president of Manna Music, of Doris Akers (Sweet, Sweet Spirit), Audrey Mieir (His Name Is Wonderful), Andraé Crouch (Through It All), and Stuart K. Hine (How Great Thou Art).

Gloria Gaither invited Judy to Nashville in 1992 where the Gaithers were taping favorite songs and singers. No one could have imagined the impact that the Gaither Video Series was about to make, not only for audiences, but also for the Homecoming Friends who really got to know each other during taping. In 1999, Judy married Rex Nelon with a host of these friends present. The Gaither Vocal Band, Jake Hess, Janet Paschal, Johnny Minick, and the Geron Davis Trio sang, Gloria spoke, and Amos Dodge officiated. Lifetime friend Howard Goodman escorted Judy down the aisle. Only ten months later, while in England for the taping of the *London Homecoming* video, these friends would be there to comfort Judy as Rex left this shore for heaven's.

Judy says: "That's what this music is all about, living and dying. It is our hope and belief in the future that makes us go on." Today, Judy lives in Nashville, where she continues her publishing, serves as the first woman president of the Southern Gospel Music Guild, is on the GMA and SGMA Board of Directors. She will quickly tell you — what she loves most is being a mom and grandma.

— Lou Wills Hildreth

**JANUARY 19, 1932 - JANUARY 23, 2000**

# REX NELON

*Rex was instrumental in launching the careers of his daughter Kelly, Janet Paschal, Karen Peck, and Charlotte Ritchie.*

Inducted into the Southern Gospel Music Hall of Fame, Rex expressed gratitude for having the chance to do the music he loved. Rex joined the legendary LeFevres in 1957. Later, when they became the Rex Nelon Singers, his daughter, Kelly and son, Todd, joined the group along with other new, young talent. Janet Paschal didn't show up for the first concert and telephoned Rex explaining that she had gone the wrong way on the freeway. He told her: "Janet, you are fired." He was kidding and had a reputation for being a prankster. After Janet, came Karen Peck, Charlotte Ritchie, and others. Rex collected songs and became an outstanding publisher with copyrights to songs such as: "What a Savior," and "If We Never Meet Again."

In 1999, Rex retired but was happy to get on the Gaither Homecoming touring bus when Bill invited him to sing bass at the concerts. Rex enjoyed breakfast with Bill Gaither, Jake Hess, Bob Cain, Ben Speer, and others where they reminisced and all agreed: "These are the good ole days."

These friends were with us when we married, and in too short a time they would be there again to bring comfort when Rex passed away, just hours before the taping of the *London Homecoming*. On that video, if you look carefully, you will notice the grief on the faces of friends who have just lost one they love; yet, you can also hear the singers' song of hope concerning the future we believe in and the one who holds the future. Rex Nelon ran his race well, and he finished well. He had started with a song, and he ended his race still singing about the Lord he loved. We miss him, but we know that we will hear him singing again soon.

— Judy Spencer Nelon

www.rexnelon.com

# How Great Thou Art

Stuart K. Hine, 1953

1. O Lord my God! when I in awe-some won - der
2. When through the woods and for - est glades I wan - der,
3. And when I think that God, his Son not spar - ing,
4. When Christ shall come with shout of ac - cla - ma - tion

con - sid - er all the worlds thy hands have made,
and hear the birds sing sweet - ly in the trees;
sent him to die, I scarce can take it in;
and take me home, what joy shall fill my heart.

I see the stars, I hear the roll - ing thun - der,
when I look down from loft - y moun-tain gran - deur
that on the cross, my bur - den glad - ly bear - ing,
Then I shall bow in hum - ble ad - o - ra - tion,

thy power through - out the un - i - verse dis - played.
and hear the brook, and feel the gen - tle breeze;
he bled and died to take a - way my sin;
and there pro - claim, my God, how great thou art!

*Refrain*

Then sings my soul, my Sav - ior God to thee; how great thou art, how great thou art! Then sings my soul, my Sav-ior God to thee; how great thou art, how great thou art!

STUART K. HINE was born in 1899 in England. His parents were at that time worshipping with the Salvation Army, and dedicated him to God during a time when opposition was strong against those who proclaimed Christ.

After serving in the armed forces, Mr. Hine was called to the mission field. For many years he served in Poland and Czechoslovakia. It was during missionary work in these countries that Mr. Hine composed many of the songs for which he is well-known today, including "How Great Thou Art."

Stuart K. Hine died in 1989. The Stuart K. Hine Trust continues to support many missionary projects, with a large portion going to the Wycliffe Bible Translators.

**OCTOBER 28, 1929 -**
· · · · · · · · · · · · · · · · · · · · · · · · · · · · · · · · · · · · · · · · · · · · · · ·

# CALVIN NEWTON

*Calvin has been blessed with a loving family and friends who have been steadfast in tough times.*

Wesley Calvin Newton was born in West Frankfort, Illinois. His father was a pentecostal preacher who was continuously looking for work. Although his family's frequent moves were hard on young Calvin, he found that singing in church was as natural as talking. By the time he was six, he was singing with his mom and dad on a Saturday morning radio show in Harrisburg, Illinois.

In the 1940s, employment opportunities abounded, and the family moved to Chicago. Calvin worked at night unloading boxcars as the supervisor of grown men. In high school, Calvin constantly got into fights. At that time, his parents sent him to a boarding school in Sevierville, Tennessee. His love for gospel music took root while he sang at one of the finest gospel finishing schools.

Calvin joined the Melody Masters along with Jake Hess, "Big Chief" Wetherington, and Wally Varner. He was still in his teens when the number one gospel group, the Blackwood Brothers, came knocking on his door.

Calvin was honored as a past member of the Oak Ridge Boys when the group was inducted into the GMA Hall of Fame. He was presented the Living Legend Award by Grand Old Gospel Reunion. He has been married to Joyce since 1963. They have two children, son, Wes, and daughter, Jackie Newton Harling. Jackie had a solo on the *New Orleans Homecoming* video. Calvin and Joyce also have a granddaughter, Samantha.

It meant a lot to Calvin when Jake Hess visited him while he was in prison and stood by him when he felt abandoned. Later Bill Gaither invited him to be a part of the Homecoming videos and many people have been touched by his testimony. Now Calvin's favorite song is "Something Beautiful."

210

# DOUG OLDHAM

*At age eight, Doug sang "The Holy City" and was paid a silver dollar, which he still has.*

From the time his father, Dale Oldham, stood him on a table at a National Youth Convention, Doug has been singing. His first paid performance was at age eight. He sang "The Holy City," and Bill Peak gave him a silver dollar, which he still has. His inspiration to sing came from Herb Thompson, his hero. He is called "gospel's great communicator." Doug's lifelong striving to make the words meaningful came from Dr. Robert Nicholson, who gave him one verse to sing with the Anderson College Choir. The song was "My Soul Is Satisfied," verse four. It set his sail.

Doug has traveled the world singing. He also has been on Christian television for decades. Doug has appeared at the White House, Carnegie Hall, Wolftrap, the SuperDome, Hines Hall, Praise Gathering, Christian Artists Seminar, CBA, NRB, Benny Hinn, and on Gaither Homecoming videos. He has sung for five presidents as well as the Queen of England and Prince Philip.

Doug has hosted three TV shows, written two books, one with his wife, Laura Lee. He has recorded sixty-five albums, one of which went gold. The albums have recently been remastered and put on CDs. Doug has also received two Dove Awards and two Angel Awards. With all of these accomplishments, his family is his heart's joy.

Doug's personal testimony could be stated in three Gaither songs: "The Old Rugged Cross Made the Difference," "Thanks to Calvary," and "He Touched Me." His favorite verse of scripture is Romans 8:28.

Doug and Laura Lee have been married since 1951. They have three daughters, three sons-in-law, and five grandchildren. All are Christians and serving the Lord. This is Doug Oldham's legacy.

— Laura Lee Oldham

www.dougoldham.com

212

**APRIL 28, 1919 - NOVEMBER 6, 1986**

# DOY OTT

*Doy's smooth baritone voice helped to make the Statesmen what many consider to be the best quartet overall in southern gospel history.*

**D**oy Willis Ott fell in love with southern gospel music when he first heard the Virgil Stamps Quartet on a broadcast from radio KRLD in Dallas, Texas. A career as a musician, singer, and vocal arranger was the result of this influence. Doy played for a string of groups including the Stamps-Baxter Quartet, the Melody Boys, the Hartford Quartet, and the Rangers with Arnold Hyles, Vernon Hyles, Walter Leverett, and Denver Crumpler. He also played the piano for the Homeland Harmony Quartet before being invited to play for the famous Statesmen Quartet while Hovie Lister was away serving in the Korean War. When Hovie returned, Doy became the group's permanent baritone singer.

Hovie always appreciated Doy's versatility as an arranger and pianist. On stage the most lively moment for the Statesmen Quartet would come when they sang their rousing spiritual, "Get Away Jordan." Hovie would jump up from the piano, Doy would slip onto the piano bench, and "Hovie Lister and the sensational Statesmen would bring down the house." (As they say in these circles.) Doy always had a smile on his face and was a quiet-natured man with a kind word. He contributed much to the success of the Statesmen during the more than twenty-five years he spent with the group.

Doy was married to Mary and they had a son, Skipper. He was inducted into the Southern Gospel Music Association Hall of Fame in 2000.

**DECEMBER 21 -**

# IVAN PARKER

*Ivan proclaims the gospel in song across the nation in over two hundred concerts each year.*

Ivan Parker was born in Roanoke Rapids, North Carolina. He sang his first solo in church at the age of two. One Sunday night, the pastor, Ivan's father, asked, "Does anyone have a song to sing?" Immediately, Ivan jumped off his mother's lap, ran to the microphone, and began to sing, "On the wings of a snow white dove, He sends His pure, sweet love." He kept on singing until his father said, "Okay, I think that's enough." Ivan was saved in that same church when he was nine. That decision has remained steadfast throughout his life as he follows the calling to use his God-given talents to share the gospel of Jesus Christ.

Ivan says that his parents have been his greatest influences. His mother Katie always prayed that God would use her children in ministry. Ivan sees his own life as a fulfillment of his father's dreams. His father was a singer and musician who put music aside when called to the ministry. Singers who have influenced Ivan are Bill Gaither and Jake Hess. Jake called Ivan his "favorite crooner."

Ivan says that the song "It Is Well with My Soul" has often ministered to him, but that his all-time favorite song is "Midnight Cry."

Ivan has been part of fifty-eight Homecoming videos and sings on the Homecoming tour. In addition, Ivan has his own solo concert ministry.

The SGMA honored Ivan as Soloist of the Year in 1998. Ivan has been voted Favorite Lead Vocalist, six times, and Favorite Male Vocalist, eight times, by *Singing News*. In 2001, 2002, 2003, and 2004, *Singing News* fans voted Ivan, Soloist of the Year.

Ivan and his wife Teresa have two sons, Ryan and Josh.

www.ivanparker.com

216

**APRIL 4, 1948 -**

# SQUIRE PARSONS

*In 1981, Squire's song, "Sweet Beulah Land" was voted "Song of the Year" by Singing News. Many groups have recorded his songs.*

Squire Enos Parsons, Jr., was born in Newton, West Virginia. He and his wife, Linda, live in Leicester, North Carolina, and have four children. He was named after his father, Squire, and also his great-grandfather, Squire Smith. He grew up singing gospel music at home and at church where Squire, Sr. was the music leader. Squire was first influenced by the 78 rpm recordings, that his mother often played for him, of the Statesmen, the Blackwood Brothers, and the Chuck Wagon Gang. Wonderful family music continuously surrounded him at home on the mountain farm in West Virginia. Family gatherings included singing from music in the shaped-note style, which Squire, Sr. taught locally. Through the years, Squire's love of gospel music continued to grow. He went on to study music, received a bachelor of science in music education, and taught music in public schools. At the same time, he sang with the Calvarymen and then joined the Kingsmen Quartet of Asheville, North Carolina, in 1975. He left the Kingsmen in 1979 to start the solo ministry in which he is still active today.

Squire has been active not only in the performance but also in the composing of gospel music. His most popular song has been "Sweet Beulah Land" which was released in 1979 on his first solo recording. It was voted Song of the Year in 1981 by *Singing News Magazine*. Other popular songs recorded by Squire have been "He Came to Me" and "Broken Rose."

Squire has often expressed the desire that when the people leave our concerts, they will be saying, "Oh, what a Savior," rather than, "Oh, what a singer."

— Nancy Gossett

www.squireparsons.com

**OCTOBER 18 -**

# JANET PASCHAL

*Janet's family is close to her heart. She says, "My family is special to me because we seldom discuss my career. We are family first."*

**B**orn in Reidsville, North Carolina, Janet Ann Paschal grew up listening to Judy Garland and Barbra Streisand and was influenced by her family's passion for music, including her father and uncles' group the Paschal Brothers. Her desire to sing grew, and after graduating from high school, Janet began to sing professionally in pursuit of her dream.

Janet joined the Rex Nelon Singers, where her powerhouse soprano vocals became a benchmark of excellence in the gospel music world. She was greatly inspired by Rex's leadership and enjoyed many successes with the group.

Janet later spread her wings, recording her first solo album in 1988 and embarking on her own solo career. From national television appearances to becoming a mainstay on the Gaither Homecoming concert series around the world, Janet's smile and her profound ability to "bring a song vividly to life on stage" have inspired countless people.

Janet has enjoyed two Grammy nominations, three Dove nominations, and has been lauded among several top female vocalist categories of the industry. Her performances and songwriting talents have taken her from a national ceremony at the Tomb of the Unknown Soldier in Washington, D.C., to appearances alongside Billy Graham.

Janet is also known for her search for truth in life, captured in her journal writings which she organized into a book, *The Good Road*, a poetic collection of inspirations from her own life's journey. Part of that journey led Janet, in 1992, to become the official spokesperson for Mission of Mercy, an international Christian relief organization.

In 1999, Janet married commercial airline pilot, John Lanier. The two make their home in her native North Carolina.

— Celeste Winstead

www.janetpaschal.com

220

JULY 12, 1956 -

# SANDI **PATTY**

*The most awarded female vocalist in contemporary Christian music,*
*Sandi is a 2004 inductee into the GMA Hall of Fame.*

Sandra Faye Patty was only two years old when she sang her first solo. The place was the church in Oklahoma City, Oklahoma, where her father, Ron, was minister of music and her mother, Carolyn, was the church pianist. Sandi remembers growing up in church and says that she and her two younger brothers had to "sit on the front row, right in front of the piano, so my mom could keep an eye on us."

As one of the most highly acclaimed performers in our time, Sandi has received thirty-nine Dove Awards, five Grammy Awards, four Billboard Music Awards, and is a 2004 inductee into the GMA Hall of Fame. This makes her the most awarded female vocalist in contemporary Christian music history. Her albums, including three platinum and five gold, have sold more than eleven million copies.

Sandi was introduced to the nation in 1986 during the rededication of the Statue of Liberty when her rendition of "The Star Spangled Banner" was broadcast on ABC's Liberty Weekend special.

In the early days of her career, more than two decades ago, Sandi traveled extensively with the Bill Gaither Trio. It was there that she learned some invaluable lessons about the importance of recreating feelings for the audience.

Today, Sandi says that she is honored, humbled, and grateful to sing in congregations across the country. She further states, "If I can encourage people in their journey with Christ, if I can challenge them to draw closer to the Lord, that is what I want my music to do."

www.sandipatty.com

**OCTOBER 20, 1926 - OCTOBER 15, 1999**

# GLEN PAYNE

*As lead singer for the Cathedrals, Glen was voted Favorite Lead Singer three years in a row by Singing News fans.*

Glen Weldon Payne was born in Royse City, Texas. His love for gospel music began at an early age. When he was seven, his grandfather took him to hear V. O. Stamps and his quartet. For Glen, it was an unforgettable experience. From that time, he knew what he wanted to do with his life. He attended the Stamps School of Music for four years beginning in 1939. The fundamentals learned there laid the foundation for a career that lasted nearly sixty years.

After a stint in the army, Glen returned to teach in the Stamps School of Music. While there, he sang with two quartets, the Frank Stamps Quartet and the Stamps-Ozark Quartet. In January, 1957, he joined the Weatherfords. In August, 1963, Glen formed a trio to sing for the Cathedral of Tomorrow in Akron, Ohio. Members included Bobby Clark and Danny Coker. After a year and a half, the trio became a quartet. Eventually, Glen co-owned the quartet with George Younce and was the manager. The Cathedral Quartet became known as the premier group in southern gospel music.

It was at the Cathedral of Tomorrow that Glen met Van Harris. They were married on November 30, 1958. Glen and Van became the parents of Carla, Todd, and Darla and have three grandchildren, Jordan, Marla, and Cole.

Over his lifetime in gospel music, Glen was nominated for eleven Grammys. As a member of the Cathedrals, he was inducted into the Gospel Music Association Hall of Fame and into the Texas Music Hall of Fame, as well as the Southern Gospel Music Hall of Fame, and the Radio Music Hall of Fame.

224

# GUY PENROD

*In 1994, after a decade of backing up others, Guy took the lead in one of the industry's most celebrated groups, the Gaither Vocal Band.*

Guy Penrod claims Abilene, Texas as his hometown. His father was a preacher in New Mexico where, at the age of three, Guy sang his first solo, "Fill My Cup, Lord." Guy remembers the church being the focus of Penrod family life, but he never really dreamed of being a musician.

Guy has a bachelor of arts degree in music from Liberty University where he attended on a music scholarship. While there, he sang with a traveling group that accompanied Jerry Falwell on his engagements.

A fellow Liberty student became his wife on the evening of graduation day. Guy's first position after graduation was teaching music in a junior high school in Atlanta. Guy says that it was a good experience but one that he would not volunteer for again.

After a move to Nashville, Guy began doing session work, singing jingles, and appearing in TNN's *Music City Tonight*. He has provided backup vocals for such artists as Amy Grant, Michael W. Smith, Larnelle Harris, Garth Brooks, James Ingram, Steve Green, and Phillips, Craig, and Dean. He also made a few appearances with the Gaither Vocal Band.

Then came a call from Bill Gaither that the Vocal Band was looking for a lead singer. In the spring of 1994, after a decade of backing up others, Guy took the lead in one of the industry's most celebrated groups.

Guy says the Vocal Band is family friendly, and he gives his boys as much "Daddy time" as possible. His wife Angie, a life-long student, according to Guy, homeschools their seven sons, Tyler, Logan, Joe, Jesse, Levi, Grayson, and Zechariah. The family likes hiking in the woods and riding horses.

OCTOBER 21, 1969 -

# DAVID PHELPS

*As a member of the highly acclaimed Gaither Vocal Band, David's spectacular voice has won the hearts of thousands.*

**B**orn in Dallas, Texas, David Norris Phelps grew up in Temball. His unusual singing talent was recognized at an early age. He knew he wanted to perform music for the glory of God. In college, David was encouraged to sing opera or on Broadway. His love for Christian music outweighed all other options. In 1988, and still in his teens, David became the youngest winner of the Seminar in the Rockies held in Estes Park, Colorado. After graduation from high school, he was the artist in residence for a church in Hurst, Texas.

By 1996, David and his wife Lori, packed up their earthly belongings and headed to Nashville to fulfill his dream of becoming a Christian artist. After six months with no job offers and their funds getting low, they made a weekend trip back to Texas. While there, his family prayed for a miracle. When they arrived back in Nashville the next day, God answered David's prayer. He heard about an opportunity with the Gaither Vocal Band. Two weeks later, he officially became a member.

With the Gaither Vocal Band, he has received four Dove Awards and two Grammy Awards. He recently released a solo project called *Revelation* with songs that he primarily wrote or co-wrote. David especially likes the first line of "Break Free" which says: "Forget what you've heard about Jesus, if it doesn't begin and end with love."

David is living his dream and reaching thousands of people with his wonderful tenor voice. His wife reminds him to honor God who gave him the talent. David is unable to pick a favorite song because there are so many.

David and Lori have four children, Callie, Maggie, Grant, and Coby.

www.davidphelps.com

## SEPTEMBER 21, 1922 -

# ROSA NELL SPEER
# POWELL

*Rosa Nell's unique style of playing the piano contributed greatly to popularity of the Speer Family.*

**B**orn in Double Springs, Alabama, Rosa Nell was the second child of Tom and Lena Speer. "Rosie" followed in the footsteps of her older brother, Brock.

The story goes that as soon as the children were talking, their father made sure they were on pitch. The Speer Family consisted of Tom "Dad" and Lena "Mom" and Tom's sister and brother-in-law, Pearl and Logan Claborn. The group needed accompaniment for the singers, so it was decided that each child would be given an instrument to play. Rosie was given the piano, and she has delighted audiences ever since with her unique style of playing.

When Dad Speer took a job with the Vaughn Music Company, the family moved to Lawrenceburg, Tennessee. In 1946, to further their music career, Dad Speer felt the family should move to Nashville. It wasn't long before Rosie met James Edwin Powell, and they were married on June 19, 1948. For the first time, a family member left the group. Rosie and Edwin started the Powell Lacey Quartet. They appeared in churches and concerts and had their own radio program from Sand Mountain, Alabama. Besides rearing three children and two step-children, Rosa Nell taught piano lessons and is still teaching young people to play. After Edwin's death in 1979, Rosa Nell and Mary Tom, also a widow, rejoined the Speers. Once again Rosie's piano playing was memorable. The Alabama Music Hall of Fame recognized her contribution to the Speer Family. Although now retired, she has appeared on several Gaither Homecoming videos.

— Faye Speer

# WESLEY PRITCHARD

*Wesley toured with Michael W. Smith and later was part of the Old Friends Quartet with Ernie Haase, George Younce, and Jake Hess.*

**K**evin Wesley Pritchard was born in Lenoir, North Carolina. He grew up in a pastor's home. Wesley says, "I never knew anything else but singing. My family has been singing all my life." A producer, arranger, and singer, in the 80s, Wesley toured with Higher Ground and Michael W. Smith. His expertise in these areas is best used at Mill West Studios, the recording studio he owns with Milton Smith.

Wesley's first solo album, *Champion of Love,* was released in 2002. The project has favorites, some new songs, and a couple that Wesley and his wife, Teresa, co-wrote.

For two years, Wesley sang with the Old Friends Quartet which included Ernie Haase and gospel legends, George Younce and Jake Hess. The quartet's first project, *Encore,* earned Wesley, as a member, his first Dove Award in 2002 for Southern Gospel Album of the Year. Wesley says, "This was one of the greatest things I have ever been involved with." Old Friends Quartet released another album, *Feelin' Fine,* in 2003.

Wesley lives in Fayetteville, North Carolina with his wife, Teresa. They have two children, Erica, who is a speech pathologist assistant and Kramer, who is studying recording technologies at Barton College.

Wesley is the worship leader at Fayetteville Community Church where he and his father are co-pastors.

Wesley's favorite song is "Going Home."

www.millweststudios.com

## MARCH 2 -

# DOTTIE RAMBO

*Dottie's songs have been recorded by Bill Gaither, Larry Gatlin, Johnny Cash, Sandi Patty, George Beverly Shea, and countless others.*

Joyce Reba Rambo, known as "Dottie," was born in Madisonville, Kentucky, and grew up in Morganfield, Kentucky. She wrote her first song at the age of eight. A fan of the Grand Ole Opry, little did she know that she would one day perform there and that her songs would be heard there and around the world.

Dottie left home at the age of twelve to enter a full-time career of singing and composing music. She was married at the age of sixteen and became a mother at eighteen. Her family became the Rambos and were known worldwide for their distinct, award-winning harmonies that set precedents in the gospel music world. Dottie has penned such classic songs as "We Shall Behold Him," "If That Isn't Love," "The Perfect Rose," "Behold the Lamb," and countless others.

Dottie has won awards including a Grammy, the ASCAP Lifetime Achievement Award, Dove Awards, and Christian Country Music Association awards. She has been inducted into the GMA Hall of Fame and the SGMA Hall of Fame, in addition to being named Songwriter of the Century.

Dottie testifies, "I grew up in a family of eleven children. My older sister, Nellie, is like a mother to me, and of course, we were always close to our mother. My father was very abusive and asked me to leave home when I was twelve because I wanted to be a gospel singer. So I left home. The rest is history. Later on his death bed, I led my father to the Lord, and he was my best friend. God has brought me through so much. God sent me a new anointing and touched me in a very special way."

— Celeste Winstead

www.dottierambo.net

234

**FEBRUARY 7, 1962 -**

# LYNDA RANDLE

*Lynda's voice has been described in the grand tradition of two of the most legendary gospel singers, Mahalia Jackson and Ethel Waters.*

Born and reared in the inner-city culture of Washington, D.C., Lynda Randle has used her early experiences to bring depth to her ministry. As the middle child of seven in a family of singers, Lynda wanted to be a cosmetologist. Her father, a part-time pastor has had great influence on her life and led her to a relationship with the Lord at age twelve. Her mother, a singer, was her first Mahalia Jackson, according to Lynda.

In the ninth grade, Lynda was sent to a Christian school in suburban Maryland where she sang in an all-white choir. Here, she really found her voice and began entering and winning regional competitions. After winning the Mahalia Jackson Award in D.C. at eighteen, Lynda was offered a music scholarship to Liberty University. When Lynda was asked to sing at various events, she always asked her audiences to pray for her, because she wanted to be the world's greatest gospel singer. In 1981, God helped her realize that her personal goal was not as important as the fact that she had his anointing.

Lynda's concert work led her to Kansas City and a youth minister, Michael Randle. Lynda sang on local television and Michael just happened to see her. They were married two years later. Just before her marriage, Lynda met Gloria Gaither at a women's conference. Lynda was invited to video tapings and also to join the Homecoming Friends in concerts. In addition, Lynda has been following a lifelong dream, speaking at women's conferences.

Lynda and Michael have two daughters, Patience and Joy. The girls are home-schooled which allows the family to travel together to Lynda's concert dates. Lynda's deep, rich voice is born out of experience and wisdom beyond her years.

www.lyndarandle.com

## FEBRUARY 17, 1931 -

# NAOMI SEGO READER

*In her fourth decade of singing gospel music, Naomi is still touring with Naomi and the Segos.*

**B**orn in Enigma, Georgia, Ruth Naomi Easters is among the five ladies credited with being the "first ladies" of gospel music. Naomi developed an interest in music at an early age. In 1949, she married James Sego and the couple moved to Macon, Georgia. James had a gospel group named the Harmony Kings. Later, the group changed its name to the Sego Brothers Quartet. During the late 1950s, they sang live every Saturday on WMAZ-TV in Macon. One day when a singer was ill, James asked Naomi if she wanted to sing on TV that day. She did and the station was flooded with calls. Naomi became a permanent member, and the group became the Sego Brothers and Naomi.

In 1958, the Sego Brothers and Naomi became known worldwide when they recorded their first album with the hit song, "Is My Lord Satisfied with Me?" People got to know the group because of this song. In 1962, they became the first group in the history of gospel music to have a million-selling record with the song, "Sorry, I Never Knew You."

The group continued to tour and record throughout the 1960s and 1970s. In the late 1970s, James passed away, but Naomi continued the ministry. When she married evangelist, Vernon Reader, the group name changed yet again to Naomi and the Segos.

Naomi continues to tour well into her fourth decade of singing gospel music. In 2001, she was inducted into the SGMA Hall of Fame. She makes regular appearances on Homecoming videos and is more in demand than ever.

**JUNE 13, 1925 -**

# MARY TOM SPEER REID

*Mary Tom took the lead part and played the mandolin during the years when she sang with the Speer Family.*

**M**ary Tom Speer was born in Double Springs, Alabama. She was the third child born to Tom and Lena Speer. In 1930, the family moved to Lawrenceburg, Tennessee, so their father could work and sing for the Vaughn Music Company. The family would sing on weekends because Tom felt very strongly that the children should be in school.

Their next move took them to Montgomery, Alabama, for a radio show. In 1946, the family moved to Nashville so that Brock and Ben could attend Trevecca Nazarene University.

During a musical event, Mary Tom met a Trevecca student and radio announcer. After a few dates, she became Mrs. Robert L. Reid on April 30, 1954. As the original alto of the Speer Family, Mary Tom continued to sing with the group until Bob finished seminary. He was a pastor in the Lutheran Church of America until he passed away in December 1968.

Mary Tom has worked as the secretary for Ben Speer Publishing Company since 1969 and helps get things organized for the Ben Speer Stamps-Baxter School of Music. She is loved and adored by students at the school where she serves as dorm mother.

Mary Tom is the mother of three children, Teri, Cyndi, and Timothy, and grandmother of six. She continues to play the piano for her Sunday school class and usually has a solo ready to sing.

Mary Tom has been featured often on Gaither Homecoming videos where Bill Gaither has said that he has received many comments about Mary Tom's smile and pleasantness.

As a member of the *First Family of Gospel Music*, Mary Tom can still hold her own with the best of vocalists. She has been inducted into the Alabama Music Hall of Fame.

— Faye Speer

240

**JUNE 23, 1974 -**

# CHARLOTTE PENHOLLOW RITCHIE

*Charlotte is thankful and truly blessed that God has given her the desires of her heart.*

**B**orn in Havre de Grace, Maryland, Charlotte Marie Penhollow considers her family special beyond words. Her parents married at a young age and gave birth to her brother Ronnie within two years of marriage. Eleven years later, Charlotte was born, followed four years later by her brother Jonathan. Despite the age gaps, the siblings are very close.

"My parents tried to spend quality time with us, making memories that would last," she explains. "My dad loves music and has been singing for as long as I can remember, and my mom is very creative. We didn't have a lot growing up, but we were loved."

Charlotte was influenced musically by her dad, Allen Penhollow, Cynthia Clawson, the Eagles, Céline Dion, Martina McBride, and Sandi Patty. Her moving soprano vocals took her on the road with the Nelons. In 1995, Jeff Easter introduced her to Greg Ritchie, the drummer for Jeff and Sheri Easter, at a Homecoming video taping. Within a year, Charlotte and Greg were married; and soon after, Charlotte began singing with the Easters.

Whether singing on stage nightly with Jeff and Sheri, on the Homecoming stage with numerous other artists, or in the studios of Nashville, Charlotte's voice has become one of the most distinctive and soothing sounds in the industry. She is known for her rendition of "Go Rest High on That Mountain," and has been nominated numerous times for Soprano of the Year. Her favorite song is "Love of God."

Charlotte and Greg make their home in Lincolnton, Georgia, and have a son, Landon, who travels with them on the bus with Jeff and Sheri Easter.

— Celeste Winstead

242

**AUGUST 29, 1928 - FEBRUARY 28, 1995**

# ROSIE ROZELL

*Through the years, Rosie thrilled his audiences with his renditions of "Hide Thou Me" and "What a Savior."*

Roland Dwayne "Rosie" Rozell was born in Hardy, Oklahoma, and became one of the premier tenors in southern gospel music. Rosie began his career with the Tulsa Trumpeteers in the mid-1950s. He attracted the attention of the Statesmen while they were touring in the area, and the group hired him in 1958. Rosie brought emotion and soul to his singing that other tenors lacked. His rendition of "What a Savior!" became a gospel classic. Audiences also were thrilled with his performances of "Hide Thou Me" and "Leave It There."

During his decade and a half with the Statesmen, Rosie helped the group remain at the top of the gospel music charts. He left the Statesmen in 1970 to form a new group known as Rosie Rozell and the Searchers. This group included Rosie's wife, Betty, and friends, Jack Toney, Mildred and Nelson LeCroy, and John and Sandy Payton. Sandy played a Hammond organ that they took on the road with them which was not only effective, but also unique and unusual for a gospel quartet. Later, Rosie enjoyed homelife with his wife and their son when they became church musicians. He returned to the Statesmen for a brief period in the mid-1970s. Then in 1981, he joined Jake Hess, Hovie Lister, J.D. Sumner, and James Blackwood as a founding member of the Masters V.

Not long after, health problems forced Rosie to leave the road. For twenty years, he had remained one of the most popular figures in gospel music. In spite of poor health, his performances retained an amazing quality and consistency. He passed away in 1995. In 1999, he was inducted into the Southern Gospel Music Association Hall of Fame.

244

**JUNE 22, 1924 -**

# BILL SHAW

*Bill won six Grammy Awards as a member of the Blackwood Brothers.*

Bill was born Edward Lamar Shaw in Lowndesville, South Carolina, not far from the Georgia state line. His mother, Minnie, and father, Edward, moved to Anderson, South Carolina, while Bill was a baby. Bill's aunt liked the song "Billy Boy" so much that she started calling her nephew "Billy." The name stuck.

Bill started playing the bass fiddle by ear and singing with his brothers-in-law, Walker and Jimmy Pickens, in churches in the area. In 1949, Bill joined a men's choral group under the leadership of John Townsend and was encouraged to study voice by notes. Later that year, he began singing with the Harmo-Knights Quartet.

Early in 1952, he joined the South Land Quartet and from April of 1952 until September, he sang with the All American Quartet. Bill joined the Blackwood Brothers in September, 1952, and while he was with them, won six Grammy awards. He left the group in October, 1973. Bill has composed several songs including: "Because of the Love of the Lord for Me," "I'm Thankful," "My Lord Goes with Me," "The Way Is the Way of the Cross," and his most requested song, "Pablo."

Bill was crowned "King of Gospel Singers" in 1958 and in 1998 recorded a CD entitled, *Bill Shaw's Gospel Favorites.*

In 1950, Bill married Wilma Pickens. They have four children, Susan, Steve, Bob, and Lori, and seven grandchildren.

**MAY 29, 1935 -**

# HAZEL SLAUGHTER

*Hazel was part of the ministry at the Cathedral of Tomorrow and with her husband, Henry, toured with the Gaithers for seven years.*

Born in Meridian, Mississippi, Hazel Myers grew up in Laurel, where she met and married Henry Slaughter. Any gift of music or singing, Hazel says, she received from her mother, Lena. Hazel grew up singing in church and participated in special singing ensembles in her high school years.

Hazel and Henry met when he and an evangelist came to her church for a summer revival series. They soon learned they were meant to sing duets together. Even before they were married, they knew the Lord had something special for them in music ministry.

They sang their songs in local churches for the first eight years of their marriage. In the early 1960s, they became part of the music ministry of the Cathedral of Tomorrow. Hazel says, "Neither of us ever planned to have the ministry that developed over the years. We just simply followed the Lord as he opened the doors of opportunity to us."

After more than four decades of gospel music ministry, the Slaughters have reached into all parts of the country. The fact that they are still in demand by an assorted group of churches nationally is proof of their strong influence on lives where and whenever they are heard.

They have recorded over twenty-four albums, received five Dove Awards, and for seven years traveled with the Bill Gaither Trio.

Hazel and Henry are the parents of two sons, David and Michael, and a daughter, Amanda. "Great Is Thy Faithfulness" is Hazel's favorite song.

All their deserved recognition and awards for achievement over these decades fade into the background, as today they present testimony and music in the fresh flow of God's Spirit in his people.

www.henryslaughter.com

248

**JANUARY 9, 1927 -**

# HENRY SLAUGHTER

*Henry has played the piano for many groups including the Imperials, the Weatherford Quartet and the Stamps-Ozark Quartet.*

Henry Thaxton Slaughter was born in Roxboro, North Carolina. His middle name came from the doctor who delivered him. His father M.T. came from a musical family. Because he was frail as a child, Henry's mother Lila encouraged him to take piano lessons and to try to excel in this area. Henry remembers his piano teacher, Mrs. Newell, and the beginnings of his love for classical music. His other influences in music came from the Oak Grove Baptist Church in Roxboro, North Carolina.

By the age of twenty, Henry had begun playing for the Stamps-Ozark Quartet. He again played for them in 1955 and 1956. In 1956 and 1957, he played for the Tulsa Trumpeteers. He later accompanied the Weatherford Quartet for a period of three years. In 1963, he became one of the original members of the Imperials.

Henry met his wife Hazel when he came to her church for a summer revival service. They were married on December 20, 1952.

In the early 1960s, Henry and Hazel were a part of the ministry at the Cathedral of Tomorrow in Akron, Ohio. From 1969 to 1976, during taping Henry and Hazel traveled with the Bill Gaither Trio.

Henry has numerous compositions to his credit including "What a Precious Friend Is He," "If the Lord Wasn't Walking by My Side," and "Then the Answer Came."

Henry received five Dove Awards for Best Gospel Instrumentalist of the Year in the 1970s. His favorite song is "Great Is Thy Faithfulness."

Henry and Hazel have three children, David, Michael, and Amanda.

www.henryslaughter.com

**JUNE 5, 1964 -**

# LADYE LOVE SMITH

*Ladye Love says that music played a part in her coming to know Christ at the early age of seven.*

Ladye Love Long was born in Memphis but grew up in Iuka, Mississippi. She was saved during a revival at age seven. She says that even then music played a part in her coming to know Christ. In the Baptist church where she grew up there was a wonderful youth choir and a band that recorded records and traveled. Their minister of music was a converted Jew. Ladye Love's older sisters and brother were in the choir and she couldn't wait to be in it. As she watched and listened, she realized there was more to it than the music, and she began hearing God's promises. She wanted that too! She walked the aisle and prayed to ask Christ to come into her heart. Her pastor asked to meet with her the next week to make sure she really understood what she had done. Later she was baptized.

Ladye graduated from the University of Mississippi with a vocal performance major, a radio and television minor, and a master's in counseling. While living in Orlando, Florida, she sang at Disney's Epcot Center in *Voices of Liberty*. She has also been a backup singer for Larnelle Harris, Sandi Patty, Lee Greenwood, and Brenda Lee.

Ladye and husband, Reggie Smith, are known internationally for their vocal expertise. Together they have performed in thirteen countries and in some of the most outstanding places in the world, among them, Super Bowl XXVI, the Kremlin, and New York City's Carnegie Hall. They have also performed for President and Mrs. Bush and for Billy Graham crusades.

In their concerts, Ladye and Reggie provide far more than just entertainment. They are also able to minister to the personal concerns of the people in attendance.

Ladye Love and Reggie are in the process of adopting a little boy, Bret, who has been with them since he was fifteen months old.

www.reggieandladyelove.com

252

# REGGIE SMITH

*Reggie sings with Gaither Homecoming concerts as well as with his wife, Ladye Love. His studio, Reggie's Attic, is in Nashville.*

R eggie Smith grew up in Moselle, just outside Hattiesburg, Mississippi. His dad was an elementary school principal and for thirty-three years was minister of music in the Baptist church the family attended. Reggie's mother played the piano and Reggie and his two brothers sang frequently. Reggie's father was also a soybean farmer on the side. Reggie vividly remembers going home after school and ball practice and heading straight to the fields to the tractor. This is also where he spent his summers. To this day he loves the country and its simplicity.

While growing up, Reggie had two loves, music and sports. He played both in the band and on the football team. When he had to choose between the two, he chose football! He played college football at Jones Junior College and later attended Delta State University on a music and football scholarship. When he transferred to the University of Mississippi, he met Ladye Love Long. Both of them toured throughout the United States and Europe with Concert Singers. Reggie also sang during college with Selah. His brother, a cousin, and a friend were a part of this group.

While living in Orlando, Florida, Reggie sang for Universal Studios and Disney, including vocals on *The Lion King* track. He also traveled with Larnelle Harris and others.

After a move to Nashville, Reggie and his best friend, Ladye Love, began dating. They were married in 1995.

Today, Reggie participates in Gaither Homecoming concerts, as well as in concerts with Ladye. Reggie is a session singer and owns a recording studio in Nashville, Reggie's Attic, where he produces music for many artists and groups.

www.reggieandladyelove.com

254

## JUNE 26, 1930 -

# BEN SPEER

*Ben is an active record producer for artists such as Anthony Burger, the Speers, the Stamps Quartet, Vern Jackson, and many others.*

Ben Lacey Speer was the youngest child born to Tom and Lena Speer. He, like the rest of the children, was born in Double Springs, Alabama. At an early age, he was showing musical talent and was playing a ukulele and standing on the end of the piano bench playing and singing. The family moved to Lawrenceburg, Tennessee, so that his dad could write songs and sing with the Vaughn Quartet. An offer for a radio program required the family to move to Montgomery, Alabama, a good move for people to hear their music. In 1946, the family moved to Nashville so that Ben and his brother, Brock, could continue their education.

In 1953, Ben married Mildred Bradley. They have three children, Stephen, Lisa, and Darien. Ben is now the proud grandfather of five. Ben sang with the family group all over Canada, the U.S. and Europe. In 1993, he resigned from the Speer Family, but not from gospel music. For the past fifteen years, he has been producing the Homeland EZ Key Soundtracks, recording five songs a month. He heads up Welcome Home Records and has his own studio in Nashville. His publishing company has published hits such as, "What a Day That Will Be," "I'm Standing on the Solid Rock" and "I'll Walk Them Golden Stairs." The latter was recorded by Elvis. Ben also heads up the Stamps-Baxter School of Music in Nashville where he teaches young and old the unique genre of southern gospel music.

Ben was inducted into the GMA Hall of Fame in 1995 and into the SGMA Hall of Fame in 1998. He is also in the Alabama Hall of Fame. He is a director for the National Quartet Convention. At present he is music director for the Gaither Homecoming Videos Series and travels with Gaither Homecoming Concerts.

— Faye Speer

**DECEMBER 28, 1920 - MARCH 29, 1999**

# BROCK SPEER

*Brock sang to crowds as large as 200,000 at Explo 72 and to church congregations of less than a hundred.*

Jackson Brock Speer was born in Winston County, Alabama. Just two months later, his father and mother began a singing group called the Speer Quartet. For the remaining seventy-eight years, his life was inextricably intertwined with that of the group. He sang with his family his entire life with only one interruption, World War II. When the family began their career, they traveled by horse and buggy, moved up to a Model T Ford and later, to a customized bus as they traveled over 100,000 miles annually until retirement in 1998.

Brock sang to crowds as large as 200,000 at Explo 72 and to church congregations of less than a hundred; to President Jimmy Carter on the White House lawn and to untold millions over radio, television, and through recordings. His group recorded some seventy albums, won fourteen Dove Awards, and received seven Grammy nominations.

A 1950 graduate of Trevecca with a bachelor's degree in theology, he also earned a master of divinity from Vanderbilt University. In 1997, he was recognized with an honorary doctor of music by Trevecca Nazarene University.

In 1998, the Speers were inducted into the GMA Hall of Fame, the first year groups were allowed. They were the only group to ever receive the GMA Lifetime Achievement Award. Brock was past president, chairman of the board, and a permanent board member of the Gospel Music Association.

But above and beyond all that, he was married to his "darling wife, Faye" for fifty years and earned the love and fierce devotion of his children, Suzan, Marc, and Brian.

*This is a portion of the words written by Brock's nephew, Steve Speer, for Brock's funeral bulletin, April 1, 1999.*

## OCTOBER 19, 1928 -

# FAYE SPEER

*As a performer, Brock would introduce her on stage as, "my lovely wife Faye," and for over fifty years she was part of the famous Speer Family.*

Faye Ihrig Speer was born in Augusta, Kentucky, to a Nazarene preacher and his wife. Her parents provided a strong foundation and taught her the importance of family, hard work, sacrifice, and honesty. These basic principles developed into a practical, no nonsense approach to living for Faye. She says, "Two things I have learned in life are that God never fails and that we all go through changes." Plain talk by a woman who has experienced the good and sad changes in life and recognizes that the steady hand of God is always near.

Faye was in her sophomore year in college singing alto in a girl's trio when she first laid eyes on Brock Speer. She says, "I knew he was the one for me. We fell in love and married — then my life really shifted into high gear!" The honeymoon was done quartet style. With family in tow, they headed to perform at an all-night singing.

Faye sang with the group until their children, Suzan, Marc, and Brian came along. In the 1960s, she returned to the group when Dad and Mom Speer's health began to falter. During this time, she was able to complete her bachelor of science degree at Trevecca Nazarene University.

"My relationship with the Lord has been especially close since I lost Brock in 1999. I have always heard of peace that passeth all understanding, and now I know about it first hand," says Faye.

The Speers have recorded seventy albums. The group and group members have won fourteen Dove Awards and have had seven Grammy nominations. Faye was recognized with a Living Legend Award from Grand Ole Gospel Reunion. She has sung many songs over the years, but her favorite is "He Is Ever Interceding."

— Suzan Speer

## NOVEMBER 4, 1899 - OCTOBER 6, 1967

# LENA "MOM" SPEER

*Lena's beautiful soprano voice added greatly to the Speer sound. Tom thought it the voice of an angel.*

Lena Darling Brock was born in a two-room cabin at the foot of Shady Grove Hill in Cullman County, Alabama. There were two brothers and two sisters to welcome her. Her father, Dwight Brock, was one of the county's leading musicians and music school teachers. So Lena's musical education literally began in the cradle. Lena's father was an instructor for the Vaughn Music Company and Lena often played the pump organ while he taught.

All day singings were a favorite form of entertainment especially in the summer. Lena's dad had a tremendous bass voice which he put to good use in the singings. One Sunday the family piled in the family wagon for a singing in Leoma, Tennessee. There Lena met the love of her life. When Tom first heard her singing, he thought it must be the voice of an angel.

On February 27, 1920, a beautiful duet was formed. Lena had a beautiful soprano voice that added greatly to the Speer sound. The group known as the Speer Family was formed in 1921, consisting of Tom, Lena, Tom's sister, and brother-in-law. As children were born to Tom and Lena, they were given parts and taught to read music. Brock, Rosa Nell, Mary Tom, and Ben soon learned that some things are not an option. You sang and you did it correctly. Tom had a reputation for expecting every note to be sung exactly right.

The Speers, as a mixed group, have received eight Dove Awards, as well as the Gospel Music Association Lifetime Achievement Award. Lena and Tom were among the very first to be inducted into the GMA Hall of Fame.

Lena and Tom were pioneers in gospel music. They began a ministry that became a meaningful way to tell the story of salvation, and the message captured the hearts of those who heard it.

— Faye Speer

**MARCH 10, 1891 - SEPTEMBER 7, 1966**

# Tom "Dad" Speer

*In Tom's family, after chores were done in the evening, they would gather to sing around the old pump organ.*

George Thomas Speer was born in Fayette County, Georgia, to a poor cotton farmer. He was the fourth child in a family that eventually numbered eighteen. Everyone worked; education was not a priority. Tom finally finished the seventh grade at the age of twenty-five. His education didn't stop there because he was an avid reader of the Bible and other books that he thought worthwhile.

Tom's first musical influence came from his home. After all of the chores were done, many nights, the family would sing around the old pump organ. People soon noticed that Tom had a special quality to his voice. In 1917, he was called for service in World War I. He was a lonely soldier and realized that others felt the same way he did, so he soon was leading the men in singing. He spent a year in France. The day he arrived home he headed for a *singing*.

On February 27, 1920, Tom married Lena Darling Brock. He liked to say, "I met a singer's daughter at a singing convention, got married in a singer's home, and raised a singing family."

Tom and Lena taught singing schools and went to singing conventions. Many times they were paid for their teaching with chickens, eggs, or whatever produce the farmers had.

Four children were born to form the singing group, Brock, Rosa Nell, Mary Tom, and Ben.

Tom wrote over five hundred songs in his lifetime and many have become standards in gospel music. "Heaven's Jubilee," "Sweeter Each Day," and "Old Daniel Prayed" are just a few.

With the Speer Family, Tom Speer was inducted into the Gospel Music Association Hall of Fame.

— Faye Speer

**FEBRUARY 14, 1914 - DECEMBER 30, 1993**

# IRA STANPHILL

*Ira wrote over five hundred songs including "Mansion Over the Hilltop" and "I Know Who Holds Tomorrow."*

Ira Forest Stanphill was born in 1914 in Belleville, New Mexico, and gave his life to the Lord when he was twelve years old. Three years later, he auditioned for a radio program in Coffeyville, Kansas. Young Ira won by playing his ukulele and singing popular songs of the day. His pastor suggested that Ira switch to gospel songs. The station manager agreed with the change, and this became the most popular program.

While still in high school, Ira started writing music and won honors in state-wide competitions. He studied harmony and music composition in college and traveled with a couple of evangelists.

Ira and Gloria Holloway were married in 1951 and have two daughters, Judy and Cathy. That same year, MGM offered him a recording contract, but he chose to remain in Christian work.

John T. Benson and Pat Zondervan have published over 360 of the 500 songs that Ira wrote. In 1998, Robert Duvall sang "I Know Who Holds Tomorrow" in the movie *The Apostle*. Leann Rimes sold four million recordings of this song. Other favorites include "Mansion Over the Hilltop," "Suppertime," "Unworthy," and "Follow Me."

When Ira visited lepers in Liberia, the lepers sang to him. Gospel music crossed denominational lines when Catholic nuns in Poland sang his song, "Mansion Over the Hilltop."

In the late 1950s, Ira sang in Royal Albert Hall in London at the Easter season. The venue might be a large auditorium or a mud hut in Africa. It didn't matter; Ira loved singing about his Savior.

*This biography of Ira was prepared by his wife, Gloria, for the Southern Gospel Music Association Award Banquet in 2001.*

# OCTOBER 12, 1934 -

# DERRELL STEWART

*Derrell's piano style has influenced many in the gospel music genre.*
*He has been a valued member of the Florida Boys since 1956.*

Derrell Martin Stewart was born in the coastal town of Brunswick, Georgia. His father was a promoter of gospel music and Derrell's mother encouraged him to start studying piano at the age of five. As a child Derrell didn't like to practice in front of other kids, so he had a plan. At home he would "run the clock up so mama would send me to school early and I could practice before anyone got there." He learned as much as he could, and later studied under James D. Walbert in Birmingham, Alabama.

Just out of high school, Derrell joined Dixie Rhythm Quartet. During this time, besides developing his unique style of playing and singing, Derrell began wearing red socks as part of his trademark. He joined the Florida Boys in February of 1956. Besides gospel, Derrell loves the big band and classical music styles.

Derrell has inspired other pianists, such as Roger Bennett and Anthony Burger. He was one of the first to receive the *Singing News* Favorite Musician Award. In 1997, he was placed on the Piano Roll of Honor at the Grand Ole' Gospel Reunion. *Singing News* surprised him by having his picture on the cover of the May, 2002 issue.

When he's at home, Derrell likes to play the baby grand piano his wife, Reve, gave him one year for Christmas. He and Reve like to visit flea markets on the lookout for treasures. Recently they found an old pump organ that they brought home, cleaned up, and polished. Derrell gets a kick out of playing it.

Derrell says that Reve takes good care of him and even washes his red socks every Monday. He hopes that his humor and playing lift the spirits of the people and that they remember to keep Christ in the center of their lives.

www.floridaboys.com

## AUGUST 3, 1924 -

# GORDON STOKER

*Gordon was an original member of the Jordanaires when they were the back-up singers for Elvis Presley.*

Hugh Gordon Stoker was born in the small town of Gleason, Tennessee, in the telephone office building where his family made their home. His mother, Willie, was the night operator and his dad, Ambus, known locally as H.A., was the repairman.

Gordon remembers playing an old Kimball organ when he was eight years old for the Jolley Springs Baptist Church with only the light from a coal oil lamp. He was called Hugh Gordon and was known, among singing circles, for his talented piano playing for the Clement Trio. Mr. Clement introduced him by saying, "He's not a banker, he's not a broker, he just the world's greatest piano player, Hugh Gordon Stoker!"

John Daniel, of the Daniel Quartet, was so impressed with twelve-year-old Hugh Gordon that he wanted to take him to Nashville to make him a star. For two years he appeared with the quartet on Radio WSM morning programs and the Grand Ole Opry. After serving three years in the Army Air Corps during World War II, Gordon enrolled at Oklahoma Baptist University. In 1948, he moved back to Tennessee to continue his studies at Peabody College. He played for the Daniel Quartet for another year until an opportunity came knocking when the Jordanaires came to town. Shortly after that, Gordon met his wife, as well as a young man who would change his life forever, Elvis Presley.

For over fifty years, the Jordanaires have been known worldwide as one of the most versatile quartets. Their background harmony style became an integral part of hit records by Elvis, Patsy Cline, and Ricky Nelson. With the Jordanaires, Gordon was inducted into the GMA Hall of Fame, as well as the Country Music Hall of Fame and was awarded several Grammys.

www.jordanaires.com

# DONNIE SUMNER

*Donnie's song, "The Night before Easter" earned him the Dove Award for Song of the Year in 1970.*

**D**onnie was born Marvin Howard in Lakeland, Florida. His father was killed when Donnie was just a young boy and Rev. Russell H. Sumner adopted him and renamed him "Donnie." Russell was J. D. Sumner's brother. Donnie was influenced by J. D., Roger McDuff, and Jake Hess. He has been told that he has a tear in his voice like Roger McDuff, pronounces his words like Jake Hess, and that he has the volume of James Blackwood.

In 1960, Donnie joined the Songsmen, and in 1964, he was with the Stamps Trio. In 1965, he joined the Stamps Quartet, and in 1972, he started the Tennessee Rangers. Soon after that in 1973, he joined up with Elvis Presley and Elvis renamed the group "Voice." Donnie was part of an eighteen-men entourage known as the Memphis Mafia. "Voice" was on call to sing for Elvis at any time. One night, they sang "In the Sweet By and By" eighteen times. This group also opened for Elvis' shows and performed his on-stage backup vocals.

In 1970, Donnie was nominated for a Grammy Award in the category of "Country Song of the Year" for his song, "Things That Matter." That same year, he was awarded the Dove Award for Song of the Year for his work entitled "The Night before Easter."

Less than a year before Elvis died in 1977, Donnie left "Voice" and experienced a spiritual new-birth in his faith walk with Jesus Christ. Donnie says he has retired from show business for full-time Christian service. He proclaims the good news that "in Jesus there is a new life, an abundant life, and the assurance of eternal life."

Donnie's favorite song is "In the Sweet By and By."

www.donniesumner.com

**NOVEMBER 19, 1924 - NOVEMBER 16, 1998**

# J.D. SUMNER

*"The Guinness Book of World Records" lists J.D. as the lowest bass singer of all time. His life was rich in relationships with family and*

**B**orn in Lakeland, Florida, John Daniel Sumner was the youngest of four children. His father was a share-cropper in the summer and worked the fruit groves in winter. His mother, a direct descendant of Robert E. Lee, supervised at a grapefruit canning plant. At the age of four, J.D. heard Frank Stamps sing at a camp meeting in Wimauma, Florida, and told his mother he wanted to be a bass singer.

At eleven, J.D.'s first pay was a box of candy from WLAK radio, where he sang in a quartet with his sister and cousins. A big break came in 1945, when he joined the Sunny South Quartet. A lifelong friendship developed with the group's lead singer, Jake Hess. In the late 40s and early 50s, J.D. sang with the Sunshine Boys in Wheeling, West Virginia. The group worked out of the WWVA Jamboree and in Hollywood as singing cowboys in western movies. In 1954, J.D. accepted a position with the Blackwood Brothers, who were at the top of the gospel music world.

In 1965, J.D. joined the Stamps Quartet whom he had rejuvenated after purchasing the Stamps Quartet Music Company. This group can boast the longest history of any male quartet. Their theme song, "Give the World a Smile," was carried across the United States and Europe.

"There was a lot of love between Mary and me," said J.D. of his marriage to Mary Agnes Varnador. "Miss Mary," as she was known, was a constant support as well as his business partner.

Always Elvis Presley's favorite bass singer, J.D. sang with Elvis on tour and in recording sessions.

J.D.'s rare talent and abilities lifted the entire industry of gospel music to national prominence.

— Shirley Sumner Enoch

274

# TANYA GOODMAN SYKES

*In the tradition of her famous Goodman Family, Tanya was a founding member of the Dove Award winning trio, Heirloom.*

**B**orn in Dallas, Texas, Tanya spent most of her childhood in Madisonville, Kentucky. The daughter of gospel legend, Rusty Goodman, Tanya has gospel music in her blood. At sixteen, she was traveling and performing with her family, and has been a part of the Goodman Family tradition of inspiring music ever since.

Tanya possesses an impressive vocal ability, one moment tenderly caressing a ballad, and the next, reveling in a joyous song of celebration. A regular on the Homecoming videos, she brings her special style of music that is sure to move all who hear her.

Tanya and her husband, Michael Sykes, penned the number one songs, "Prayer Warrior," and "The King of Who I Am." She has written and recorded several children's projects, among them the Grammy Award winner, *Rock-a-bye Collection* and the much acclaimed, *A Child's Gift of Lullabyes.*

Michael and Tanya make their home near Nashville, along with their daughters, Mallory and Aly. In recent years, Tanya has spent less time on the road and more time attending ballgames, recitals, and choir practice, and fulfilling what she believes is the greatest call upon her life, being a mom.

She says, "During my lifetime, I have been able to travel to so many places and meet countless precious men and women of faith. I've had opportunities to do and experience things that I only dreamed of when I was a young girl. My family is my greatest source of joy here on earth, and they are healthy and strong and seeking after God. What more could I ask? God is good, and I feel truly blessed." Tanya favorite song is "It Is Well with My Soul."

www.michaelsykes.com

276

NOVEMBER 11, 1953 -

# RUSS TAFF

*Russ has been influenced by all styles of music, and this is reflected in his recordings and concerts.*

Russ grew up in a pentecostal preacher's Missouri home and was influenced by his southern gospel, music-loving mother. He and his four brothers learned early that gospel music was the only music allowed in the Taff home. Young Russ recalls standing on the altar, balanced by his mom, singing with much passion the hymns of the church.

Moving to Arkansas in his teens, Russ began listening to contemporary Christian music for the first time. That is when he formed a band called the Sounds of Joy. He began to write songs that combined his early church influences with the music of his generation. In the late 1970s, Russ was invited to join the Imperials as lead vocalist. His own composition, "We Will Stand" became his signature song. After award-winning years with such songs as "Trumpet of Jesus," and "Praise the Lord," he left the Imperials to pursue a solo career. Over the next twenty years, Russ collected three Grammy Awards and nine Dove Awards. He has been hailed by *Billboard Magazine* as having "the single most electrifying voice in Christian music."

Early on, Bill Gaither invited Russ to be a part of the Homecoming videos on a regular basis. In July 2001, when Mark Lowry left to pursue a solo career, Bill asked Russ to become the new baritone in the Gaither Vocal Band.

Russ' eclectic taste is reflected in his live concerts and recordings including a mixture of southern gospel, rock, pop, black gospel, blues, country, and even big band. Russ and his wife, Tori, co-writer of many of his songs, have two daughters, Maddie Rose and Charlotte.

www.russtaff.com

**MARCH 28, 1989 -**

# AMBER NELON
# THOMPSON

*Amber's two solo recordings were nominated for Dove Awards making her the youngest-ever nominee.*

As the daughter of Kelly Nelon Clark and granddaughter of Rex Nelon, Amber was born in Marietta, Georgia. Singing comes naturally to this young lady. Amber fulfilled a life-long dream when her parents offered her the opportunity to sing soprano with the Nelons on a full-time basis. Not only was Amber the most obvious choice to take on this role, but she also was the most qualified.

Since making her first appearance on stage at the prestigious Dove Awards when she was only a week old, Amber has become one of the most recognized artists in gospel music. In addition to being featured on the Gaither Homecoming Kids videos, Amber recently started appearing on the Gaither Homecoming Friends videos and television series.

Amber is a seasoned recording veteran. Her two solo recordings *Show & Tell* and *Amber & Friends* were both nominated for Dove Awards by the Gospel Music Association, making her the youngest-ever nominee. Amber is active in the youth group at her home church of Grace Baptist where her parents serve on staff. She also enjoys traveling around the world singing with her family, the Nelons.

At her grandfather's memorial service, Amber touched the hearts of everyone with her tribute in song, "Amazing Grace." Amber is a third generation gospel music talent who is surely making Rex Nelon, her grandfather, proud.

— Jason Clark

www.thenelons.com

**AUGUST 24, 1933 - APRIL 15, 2004**

# JACK TONEY

*Jack composed over six hundred songs and sang with many groups. He will be remembered as one of the greatest voices of gospel music.*

Jackie Alonza Toney was born on Sand Mountain near Boaz, Alabama. His parents, Curtis and Carrie Toney, took young Jackie to the nearby Baptist church where he learned to sing the old hymns. His love for music and his natural talent were evident as he learned to play the piano, organ, guitar, mandolin and banjo. He could also sing like an angel. In the early 1950s, his favorite singer was James Blackwood, who later became his friend.

Jack began singing professionally in 1951 with the Joymakers and later joined the Prophets Quartet. He toured with the Florida Boys and the Speers, and later became the original lead singer for the Dixie Echoes. In 1963, Jack joined the Statesmen Quartet and toured with them for seventeen years.

In the early 1980s, after a number of years in radio and on television, Jack returned to southern gospel music with the Masters V. In 1985, the Stamps, with Jack as lead singer, were nominated by the Country Music Academy as Gospel Group of the Year.

Jack was a prolific songwriter penning over six hundred songs. He received a Number One Song Award for "I Will Rise Up from My Grave" from the Nashville Songwriters Association International.

In 1996, Jack received the Living Legend Award from the Grand Ole Gospel Reunion. Two years later he was honored as a member of the Statesmen Quartet when they were inducted into the Gospel Music Association Hall of Fame.

Jack enjoyed the many years he spent as part of the Gaither Homecoming family of artists and is featured on many of the videos.

He is survived by his wife, Gail, daughter, Cherie, and two granddaughters, Lauren and Alexandra. Jack will be remembered as one of the greatest voices in gospel music.

**JANUARY 13, 1926 -**

# WALLY VARNER

*Wally's piano style blended well when he played for the Homeland Harmony Quartet as well as the Blackwood Brothers Quartet.*

Born in Winter Haven, Florida, Wallace Belmont Varner was one of ten children. His dad, Jesse, was a singing convention school teacher, and he picked Wally out to play the piano. An old upright piano was purchased for Wally and, as it turned out, he had a natural talent for the instrument.

At seventeen, during World War II, Wally joined the navy. After the war, he played for the Melody Masters Quartet for a couple of years. From 1949 until 1955, Wally's piano style blended well as he played for the Homeland Harmony Quartet. The next group Wally joined was the Revelaires Quartet in 1956. He had a year with the Deep South Quartet in 1957 before joining the Blackwood Brothers for five years.

Many of the awards to which we are accustomed today were not given prior to 1963. Wally's awards came later. He has been recognized with the Living Legend Award, Gospel Music Piano Roll of Honor, and Gospel Music Association Hall of Fame with the Blackwood Brothers.

Wally's compositions, "Crown Him King" and "Bell of Joy Keep Ringing," have been recognized as masterpieces.

Wally and his wife Polly, have two daughters, Dale and Debbie. They have four grandchildren and four great-grandchildren. He and Polly own Varner Music, Incorporated in Winter Haven, Florida.

The songs most requested for Wally to play are "How Great Thou Art" and "Amazing Grace." There are too many songs that Wally loves to be able to pick out a favorite. His ministry's motto is "Spreading the Word thru Song" and he has accomplished this for over seventy years.

varnermusic@msn.com or 1-800-756-9551

## DECEMBER 31, 1976 -

# JASON WALDROUP

*Jason sings with Greater Vision and received the Tenor of the Year Award in 2004 during the Singing News Fan Awards.*

The 1995 National Quartet Convention changed the life of an eighteen-year-old from Opelika, Alabama, forever. It was there that Jason Waldroup stood in a stairwell at the Louisville Convention and Expo Center and sang his favorite song, "Victory in Jesus," a cappella for Gerald Wolfe and Rodney Griffin of Greater Vision.

While growing up, Jason enjoyed listening to the sounds of the Cathedrals and Gold City, and when Gerald Wolfe offered him the dream job of singing tenor with Greater Vision, he said "Yes!" "No one else in my family sings, so I learned the style of southern gospel music from listening to the groups on the radio. I loved the music, especially Greater Vision. It was truly a dream come true to be a member of this fine group."

Jason Waldroup was saved at the age of fifteen during a revival meeting that his pastor was preaching. He has enjoyed numerous awards and moments with Greater Vision including number one hits, fan awards, historic appearances, and unbelievable accomplishments.

A fact most fans don't know is that before joining Greater Vision, Jason sang in a part-time group called Faith and Believers for six months. He has been with Greater Vision since 1995. During that time fans have honored him with Favorite Young Artist and in 2004 presented him the Tenor of the Year award during the Singing News Fan Awards.

Jason now makes his home in Morristown, Tennessee, with his wife, Missy, and daughter Abigail.

— Crystal Burchett

www.greatervisionmusic.com

**OCTOBER 10, 1922 - JUNE 19, 1992**

# EARL WEATHERFORD

*As a young person, Earl attended singing schools and developed his own ideas about proper quartet singing and later mentored young talent.*

Earl Weatherford was a native of Paoli, Oklahoma. Every afternoon he would hurry home from school, turn on the radio, and listen to the Frank Stamps Quartet. Earl was partial to male quartets. His favorites were the Homeland Harmony and the Blackwood Brothers. It was not unusual for Earl to walk five miles to attend a singing convention on a Sunday afternoon. In those days, singing conventions were common events. The conventions emphasized tight harmonies and the blending of voices. Earl learned much from attending these conventions and developed his own ideas about proper quartet singing.

During World War II, Earl moved to California to work in the shipyards. While there in 1944, he organized the Gospel Harmony Boys to sing for a gospel radio show on a local station. Over the years the Weatherfords mentored young talent including Glen Payne, George Younce, Armond Morales, and Henry Slaughter.

It was at a singing convention that Earl met the beautiful sixteen-year-old Lily Fern Goble. She would have a major influence on the future of his group. Earl and Lily were married in 1945, and eventually Lily became a permanent member of the group. After many location and personnel changes, the Weatherfords found a home in Akron, Ohio, with the Cathedral of Tomorrow. As that work grew and required a group to be on staff full time, the Weatherfords chose to continue their traveling ministry. Two children joined the Weatherford family and son, Steve, took an interest in the quartet. When a baritone singer got sick, Steve begged for a chance to sing.

A life of touring took its toll, and in 1992 Earl died of congestive heart failure. With the help of others, Lily and Steve have continued in music ministry, making the Weatherfords one of the oldest groups still traveling with original members.

288

**NOVEMBER 25, 1928 -**

# LILY FERN **WEATHERFORD**

*Lily is a part of one of the oldest gospel groups still traveling with original members.*

Lily Fern Goble was born in Bethany, Oklahoma, into a very strict Nazarene preacher's family. At the age of four, her family moved to Los Angeles. Lily Fern attended a few Sunday afternoon singing schools. She remembers that many of the churches in California used Vaughan and Stamps-Baxter books as their regular hymnals. Because of her Nazarene connection, Lily was familiar with mixed groups such as the Speers, but this was her introduction to quartet-style gospel music. One afternoon in 1944, when she was only sixteen, Lily met the tall, dark, and handsome Earl Weatherford at a singing school.

Lily and Earl hit it off and were married in 1945. Earl was a master singer and patient teacher. He taught Lily to sing with "heavier tones" and to "blend with men." They did not know at the time that he was preparing her for a future career with the Weatherfords. At first Lily filled in only occasionally until a new member was chosen. Eventually, she asked Earl to let her sing as a permanent member.

In 1949, the group began to travel full time in a first class manner with a 1948 Buick pulling a one-wheel trailer. With no definite destination, the Weatherfords landed in Fort Wayne, Indiana, at radio station WOWO. As a 50,000 clear channel station with a nationwide reach, WOWO literally introduced the Weatherfords to America.

After a stint at the Cathedral of Tomorrow, the Weatherfords took to the road again full time. Earl passed away in 1992. Today Lily and son, Steve, are keeping the family legacy alive in full-time music ministry.

www.lilyweatherford.com

**OCTOBER 31, 1922 - OCTOBER 2, 1973**

# JAMES "BIG CHIEF" WETHERINGTON

*Big Chief was considered one of southern gospel's greatest bass singers. He was a key member of the Statesmen Quartet for twenty-four years.*

Because of his Native-American heritage, Hovie Lister and Lee Roy Abernathy suggested that James Stephen Wetherington should be called "Big Chief." Reared in Ty Ty, Georgia, Chief began his career with the Sunny South Quartet, and later sang with the Melody Masters. Big Chief served with honor in the United States Navy during World War II.

After the war, he joined the legendary Statesmen Quartet that placed him as one of the greatest bass singers of all time. He later moved to Atlanta and directed the choir at the Assembly of God Tabernacle, when he was not on tour with the Statesmen.

Big Chief sometimes stirred up church audiences with his onstage shaking that some considered lewd. It has been noted that Elvis Presley patterned his style of movement directly after Big Chief and his singing style from another Statesmen, Jake Hess.

With his partners, Hovie Lister and Doy Ott, Big Chief owned Faith Publishing Company and J. M. Henson Publishing Company, as well as the Statesmen Quartet. Wetherington also owned the Lodo Music Company.

Big Chief died just before his fifty-first birthday as a result of a heart attack suffered in his hotel room in Nashville. He had been appearing at the National Quartet Convention, an event he was instrumental in helping J. D. Sumner start. He was inducted into the Southern Gospel Music Hall of Fame in 1997.

292

**APRIL 1, 1963 -**

# GERALD WOLFE

*Gerald has received the Male Vocalist Award for four years. He sings with the highly-acclaimed group, Greater Vision.*

**G**erald Wolfe was born in Morristown, Tennessee. At age eight, Gerald accepted Christ as his personal Savior at a Wednesday night revival meeting. He received his love for music from listening to his mother, Mary, play the piano in their church, as well as for the church quartet. Gerald says, "She always wanted me to sing and would buy sheet music of new songs for me to learn for church. My mom always encouraged me to play and learn shaped note music, which I still use today. Both my parents loved and still love gospel music. I grew up going to concerts and Saturday night singings all over east Tennessee. The groups that had the greatest influence on me would be the Happy Goodman Family, the Le Fevres, the Speers, and the Cathedral Quartet."

Gerald fueled his desire for gospel music by packing his bags and traveling on the road. Gerald started his journey with the Dumplin Valley Boys in 1981, then the Dumplin Valley Trio in 1986. He soon took the stage with one of his favorite groups, the Cathedrals, from 1986 to 1988. He toured as a soloist from 1989 to 1990 and now nightly takes the stage with Greater Vision, a group he helped form.

Gerald has received many awards including Favorite Newcomer in 1987, Favorite Young Artist in 1988, and Male Vocalist in 2000, 2001, 2002, 2003, along with numerous group awards. Greater Vision has held continuous number one spots on the Christian charts for songs such as "My Name Is Lazarus," "He's Still Waiting by the Well," and "Just One More Soul." Gerald says, "You'll never get to hear my favorite song I have composed!" His favorite song to sing is "There Is a River."

Today, Gerald and his wife, Donna, still make their home in Morristown, Tennessee, with their children, Benjamin, Avery, and Casey.

— Crystal Burchett

www.greatervisionmusic.com

# Woody Wright

*Woody was awarded the Christian Country Song of the Year for "Ever Since I Gave My Heart to You."*

Woodrow Wilson Wright was born into a musical family in Cleveland, Tennessee. His dad, Woody, Sr., was a bluegrass musician and sang baritone in a gospel quartet called the Dixieaires. Growing up in a small town, Woody was an active member of the Cedar Grove Baptist Church and part of the one-hundred voice youth choir.

In high school, Woody formed his own gospel group called the Woody Wright Singers and traveled around the South singing in churches. Growing up in this environment gave him the Christian foundation that has been a solid source of encouragement through various Christian and secular endeavors.

Woody was influenced musically by Flatt & Scruggs, Jake Hess, Larry Gatlin, the Oak Ridge Boys, James Taylor, Kris Kristofferson, the Little River Band, and the Homecoming Friends.

Some of the groups with whom Woody has participated are the Scenicland Boys; Willie Winn & the Tennesseans; Memphis; Ponder, Sykes, & Wright; Matthew Wright & King; and the Prime Time Country Singers.

Woody's compositions have been nominated for awards by the Academy of Country Music and the Gospel Music Association. His songs "I'm Gonna Sing" and "More Than Ever" have been recorded by the Gaither Vocal Band.

"I am most blessed to live in 'Small Town USA' — Alexandria, Indiana, with my beautiful wife and life partner, Yvonne (Vonnie). I have a daughter from a previous marriage, Carli, age twelve, who is a talented musician and an aspiring actress."

Woody's favorite song is "The Love of God" by F. M. Lehman.

www.woodywright.net

# GEORGE YOUNCE

*Bill and Gloria Gaither wrote the song, "Thanks to Calvary," for George.*

George Wilson Younce was born in Patterson, North Carolina, to Tom and Nellie Younce. He was the youngest of five children who realized that their baby boy was an entertainer and enjoyed being his audience. In 1945, Ike Miller invited him to join the Spiritualairs and suggested they go to Dallas to the Stamps-Baxter School of Music. George was overwhelmed but grateful when his dad went to the bank and borrowed the money. The Greyhound bus ride was lonely and he couldn't stop thinking about home until he arrived and became so busy and thrilled with the music lessons from the masters of that day. In 1954, he sang with the Watchmen and during that time he spotted Clara, the most beautiful girl. On April 27, 1955, he and Clara traveled over to Raven Cliff, West Virginia, where George paid three dollars for a license, happy that he was marrying the "coal miner's daughter."

For a short while, they moved to Atlanta where George sang with the Homeland Harmony Quartet, a job he later turned over to Rex Nelon. Earl asked him to come back to the Weatherfords and during this time he found his niche in the music business. In 1957, George joined the Blue Ridge Quartet. In 1964, he founded the award-winning Cathedral Quartet and would have success with his partner and Cathedral co-owner, Glen Payne. They were together until 1999 when they retired the Cathedral name. George has enjoyed the Homecoming videos and concerts where Bill Gaither's friends, George, Jake Hess, Ernie Haase, and Wesley Pritchard organized the Old Friends Quartet and continued to thrill audiences. Today, George is a co-founder of Ernie Haase and the Signature Sound Quartet. George and Clara have five children: Gina, Dana, Lisa, George Lane, and Tara, and three grandchildren.

— Judy Spencer Nelon

# His Name Is Wonderful

Audrey Mieir

His name is Won-der-ful, His name is Won-der-ful, His name is Won-der-ful, Je - sus, my Lord; He is the might-y King, Mas-ter of ev-ery-thing, His name is Won-der-ful, Je - sus, my Lord. He's the great Shep-herd, the Rock of all a - ges, Al-might-y God is He; Bow down be-fore Him, Love and a-dore Him, His name is Won-der-ful, Je - sus, my Lord.

# Acknowledgements

This book, *It All Started with a Song*, has been decades in the making. However, I have spent only the last year researching and drawings these giants and soon-to-be leaders in the gospel music genre. Bill Gaither said recently, about the turtle on the fence post, "It only got there with some help." In the making of this book, I have had much help and patience from my wife, Avis. I would still be working on it had she not stood by me. The technical abilities of my assistant, Tammy Burrell, have once again been vital in the production of this book. Judy Spencer Nelon shared her vast knowledge of the people in the industry and has been so very helpful in the research. The staff members at the Gaither offices have contributed much to the making of this book, especially Connie Williams, Jeralee Mathews, and Lynda Odom. Others who deserve special thanks are Christie Stephens, David Coolidge, Tina Robbins, Janet Brandon, Jim Bailey, Don Boggs, Sam Collins, Arthur Kelly, Fran Thompson, Scott Brooks, Bill and Bettye Dennis. Also, I especially want to thank the writers who contributed to the book. They are Judy Nelon, Lou Hildreth, Celeste Winstead, Crystal Burchett, Laurie Winton, Allison Stinson, Bob Crichton, Jack Williams, Gloria Stanphill, Jason Clark, Nancy Gossett, Faye Speer, Steve Speer, Suzan Speer, Bonnie Morales, Vonnie Wright, Charles deWitt, Joy MacKenzie, and Amy Grant. Family members of the featured artists contributed so much and I am truly grateful for their help. In addition, I want to thank the music publishers, Gaither Copyright Management, Gaither Music Company, Lojon Music, Life Gate Music, Manna Music, Inc., and Hamblen Music, Inc., for permission to print their songs. And last of all but certainly most importantly, I want to express my gratitude to Bill and Gloria Gaither for their encouragement and support throughout this project.

After attending the National Quartet Convention recently, I realize that I have only scratched the surface of the singing groups that are spreading the Good News in song.

— David Liverett

David Liverett is seated in front of the "storyboard" from this, his latest book, *It All Started with a Song*. David is a pen and ink illustrator and graphic artist. Each of the 140 drawings in this book took ten to twelve hours to complete and he has worked on this project for about fourteen months. David and his wife, Avis, have a son and daughter-in-law, Mark and Katie, and two beautiful grandchildren, Connor and Clare.

Photo by Dale Pickett